How To
Get Rid
Of A MAN

Dedicated to Dr. Lois Evans

My friend, you are the one who said, "Titia get that book done. We need it."

Your wise words and your never-ending encouragement are what I kept hearing in my head throughout the process of finishing this book. Until the next time…

Thank you.

How To Get Rid Of A Man

LeTitia Owens

Owens, LeTitia

How to Get Rid of a Man / LeTitia Owens / Non-Fiction / Self-Help / Relationships

ISBN: 978-0-578-85115-0

Cover Art: Percy Ray Bryant, III

Photographer: Ada Lee Photography: Tashina Calhoun

Make-Up Artist: Chyna Doll Brand: Chyna Elizabeth

Wardrobe: Melanie Ann's Boutique & K. Mills Collection

Transcriber: Karen Coleman-Clarke

Pre-Edit Formatting: Pen_Geek-Grinville, Ltd.

Substantive Editing: Adrienne Michelle Horn – I A.M. Editing, Ink

Developmental/Copy Editing & Book Formatting: Shaundale Rénā

Contributing Editor: Angela

For Hosting/Speaking Engagements:
  LeTitia Owens
  CEO/Founder Where Are You Outreach
  5057 Keller Springs Rd. Ste. #300
  Addison, TX 75001
  972.885.9296 | 214.534.4903
  www.TitiaOwensBooks.com
  www.TitiaOwens.com

Acknowledgments

Thank you, Jesus!

JWayne, my Dovey, you have supported me through this entire process. I'll never forget when I asked you, "Are you sure you are okay with this?" Your answer was, "We all have a past; you are being obedient and doing what God told you to do. Now get to writing." You gave me the freedom and the blessing to be transparent. I can't thank you enough. You have taken me as I am, and you still love me. I am honored to be your wife. I am sooooooo grateful for you. I love you, JWayne, my love.

To my children: words cannot express the love I have for you. Having you was my greatest gift. You taught me how to love and become more selfless. Being your mom has been so rewarding, and the Lord blessed me with you as a visual of His grace and mercy. You have been rooting me on and loving me through all of my figuring-it-out stages. I pray that you know how proud I am to be called Mom by you and how much I love you!!! Thank you for being the best children this side of heaven.

Jared and Kelsey, my bonus children, thank you for loving me as I am. Your dad and I are so proud of you.

Siblings: thank you for all of the support. Love you!

Mom, watching you has molded me to be the transparent person I've become. You have been a light and a support. You are consistently making sure I have what I need to be successful and do great things. I'm sure this is a lot. Just know you mean the world to me and having your heart is what brings out the best in me. I am so proud to be your daughter. I love you, Mom. Thank you, Rev., for loving my mom through the years. Thank you for lessons you didn't even know you were teaching.

Dad, even though we have done some crazy things together, I wouldn't change a thing because regardless of our past the end goal was you made sure I gave my life to Christ and that I would live for Him. The closer you were in Christ, you brought me right with you. I am truly grateful for how you have tried to be there for me whenever you could. You made yourself available even while we were miles apart. Thank you for being the best dad I could ask for. Thank you, V, for consistently reminding us to keep our eyes on Christ.

DeAnna, everyone isn't blessed to have someone like you come along and change their entire life. I asked the Lord to send a "you" my way and little did I know it would be tough but necessary. Your mentoring put accountability on blast, and your wisdom is priceless. Thank you for the impact you have had on my life. The Lord sent you right at the time my marriage was ending, and you guided the healing process. I am so grateful. Thank you for richly blessing me.

Priscilla, my sister/friend, I just appreciate you for saying yes. Your belief and support has made all the difference. We have had 20-plus years of friendship and you and Jerry have been so faithful in reminding me you are there.

Pastor Evans, you and your wife (Dr. Lois Evans) have caused me to hunger and thirst after righteousness. There are not enough thank you's for what you have done for me and my family. Your kindness has been immeasurable, and I am humbled by your generosity. I can't begin to count the number of times I've called on you, and you have been there. You have blessed me *outstandinarily*. Mrs. Evans meant so much to me. Thank you for sharing her with us. Her legacy lives on.

Mr. S, so much of this was going on around you and most things you had no idea of. I pray that although I shared so much, it clarifies any questions you may have had. Please forgive me for the role I played in our past. Thank you for giving me the best gift in the world...our children.

Kirk and Tammy: Thank you for supporting me through it all. I can't say 'thank you' enough for being there. It has been a ride, and you rode with ya' girl over 25 years. *Wow!*

Shaundale: You are a Godsend. Your push, your commitment, and your patience was what I needed. You made sure this book had the direction it needed, and I'm forever grateful. Thank you!

Percy Ray: Not many can say they have a world-renowned graphic and apparel designer in their back pocket. I have been able to count on you countless times, and your work is impeccellent!!! Thank you for providing greatness no matter how many times I change my mind. *HA!!!*

Talisha: Thank you for the time you have taken to go through the steps of helping me to get this book done. I appreciate your friendship of over 20 years. #TandT

Portia: You are stuck with me. You have the gift of patience to keep working with me on all of my projects. You are a treasure, and I'm thankful to be blessed with someone who pushes me to get it done. #TeamPortia

Elaine Garcia: You were the very first person I called on getting started. Thank you for your wisdom and guidance. You allowed me to ring your phone whenever I had questions, and I thank you!!!!

Cheryl Polote Williamson: Your encouragement is consistent, and I appreciate you for being you.

Victoria, Julia, and Sherry: We are finally here! After years of talking to you about this book and going on and on with questions and concerns, it's done. Thank you for all of the wisdom, the love, and support you consistently provide. You have never left my side. My sisters from other mothers...I love you! I hope you're ready for another one. LOL!

Special Thanks

Focus Group: Chyna Elizabeth, LaCracha Holley, Kendra Kinnie, Tinika Bell, Maggie McGee, Vickie Hughes, Theresa Cain, Sparkle Washington, Faith Anderson, and Artherene Williams. I am so grateful you all allowed me to share my journey with you. Your presence created a safe place for me to be totally transparent. Thanks to each of you.

Foreword

For the past 25 years, I have had the honor of calling LeTitia Owens my friend. She has been a consistent and trustworthy voice of wisdom in my life and, through this book, I am so thrilled to share that voice with you.

If you are tired of playing relationship games and want to challenge yourself to rise above the hindrances that have held you back from healthy relational dynamics, this book is for you. Titia has lived through the strain of marital difficulties then divorce and has now risen to tell her story candidly and authentically in a way that will entertain, challenge, and instruct each one of us. I'm so grateful for the life lessons she has personally shared with me, and I'm excited about what she is about to share with you. Each chapter is worth the read.

Enjoy,

Priscilla Shirer
Bible teacher and best-selling author

Table of Contents

Marriage is straight-up hard at times. I'll never forget when my children's father was in a relationship with another woman, and sometimes he wouldn't come home 'til late, or not at all. One weekend, my dad, his wife, and my siblings came to visit me, and I remember wondering if he was coming home the first night of their arrival. Well, he did **not** come home, and I was more embarrassed than I was anything else.

The thought of my dad knowing my husband didn't come home made me want to **lose my mind,** but I have always had too much pride to ever give anyone a reason to believe I wasn't okay. When my husband finally came home the next day, he walked in, and I spoke to him as you would expect a sister to speak to her brother.

"Heeyy."

I spoke as if I didn't know he wasn't at home all night. *This is what I'm supposed to do—just be quiet.*

I was pretty much shattered on the inside, but I thought my silence indicated that I was spiritually strong. I know you are probably saying, "Girl, ain't no way my husband can stay out all night, and I don't say or do anything." Well, that's how foolish I was. Somewhere along the way, I started to believe I was supposed to let a man do whatever he wants to do. I didn't realize I was teaching him he could do whatever he wanted to do and treat me however he wanted. I believed that if I kept my feelings from getting in the way, I could take whatever he dished out. Listen, **I was wrong!**

"Older women likewise are to be reverent in their behavior, not malicious gossips nor enslaved to much wine, teaching what is good, so that they may encourage the young women to love their husbands, to love their children, to be sensible, pure, workers at home, kind, being subject to their own husbands so that the word of God will not be dishonored." (Titus 2:3-5).

In this book, I will take you on a journey of the lessons the Lord taught me from my disobedience while becoming a wife the first time, which brought me to brokenness. Whenever you decide to obey God's Word, the Holy Spirit will enable and empower you to turn your decision(s) into humbling actions. My disobedience caused me to face enormous consequences. However, the one consequence I suffered from most was *getting rid of my man*.

I've been putting this book off since 2002. It took all this time to get to a place, right now, to commit to reliving all the sinful experiences. As soon as Mr. S and I started going through the divorce, God told me to start writing all of this down because I would have to tell everyone what I did, and I was like, "No, I can't." That's why much of this was extremely hard to share. There were things I said in this book I've never told anyone before, so let my transparency be your starting place for speaking up and sharing your truth.

Chapter 1

Let the Games Begin

I learned how to playnipulate (a word I created) from my dad but be warned. In the process of playing games, it is sometimes difficult to determine how long the game will last or when exactly the game is going to stop. If you decide that you are going to play, you must prepare for the consequences that come with it. Since I didn't understand the consequences back then, I simply dove into the unknown full-fledged.

I first met Mr. S. (the man I got rid of) at a nightclub. At the time, I was 23 and an R&B singer in a group named Ashanti, based in Minneapolis, Minnesota, together with my friends Tam and Vidra. We sang at Prince's club, Glam Slam, Fine Line, and various other night clubs in the city. One night after we performed, Mr. S. came up to me, helped me off the stage, and asked for my name and phone number. I thought to myself *I'm not giving you my phone number.* Then Tam said to me, "Girl, he's fine. You might want to go ahead and give him your number."

At her urging, I gave him another look and agreed he was both fine *and* handsome, so I did. That's when I found out he was a professional basketball player. Now, I knew nothing about basketball except Michael

Jordan. I could talk about how high Michael Jordan could jump, but that was about it.

Mr. S started calling me. At this time, Tam, Vidra, and I lived with our manager, Jeff Taube. Not only was Jeff managing us and allowing us to live with him, but he was also like a father-figure. He was always incredibly involved with what we had going on. When we told Jeff about this basketball player I'd met, he didn't like the sound of it. All he said was, "I'm not into basketball players. They are no good." He had a negative disposition from the very beginning. Of course, **I ignored that**.

Around that time, Mr. S had to go to a basketball camp. Basketball camp is where NBA players go for about two weeks with their team to practice and prepare for the season. He called me every night to try to get me to drive about an hour and a half away to visit him, but something in my mind kept saying, *I ain't going to no basketball camp*. He was both persistent and persuasive.

He would say things like, "Come hang out. We'll have a really good time here. They give us all this free stuff. We've got this hotel with all this food," to which I always responded, "No thanks."

Finally, he came back from camp, and he asked me if he could take me out. I agreed. That is where the games really began. Yes, he asked if I could go out with him, but I thought *he's a basketball player. I'm sure women are waiting in line to spend time with him just because he's a professional athlete, so he's about to experience something different. I'm not going down like the rest of them.*

Mr. S came to the apartment and waited for me to come outside. He kept calling to let me know he was there and blowing his horn, but I purposely didn't answer the phone. I knew he was out there; I could see out my window, but I let him wait and wait for hours until he finally got upset and left. I wanted him to feel me standing him up. I wanted to know what his reaction was going to be. I was playing a game.

Later, he called me back and said, "Hey, I was waiting on you for hours out there. Where were you?"

I didn't know what to say but replied, "I must have fallen asleep." Since I didn't want to tell him the truth, that was the best lie I could come up with. He was upset but wanted to go out with me again.

"Well, I'll go out with you, but my girls have to come with me."

He agreed, so I told my girlfriends, "We're going out to eat. Get ready." I knew they wouldn't leave me hanging. Tam and Vidra would never pass on a free meal, so they got dressed. Then the four of us went out to dinner, and I ordered steak and potatoes.

As soon as the steak came out, I said, "Okay, I need some sugar."

Obviously, that was strange to him because he asked, "What are you going to do with that sugar?"

"I eat sugar on my food. I'm gonna need it on my steak."

He was surprised (and I bet you are as well). However, my friends knew this about me. I eat sugar on almost everything. Later, I found out they were thinking, *he's going to think she's crazy because something has to be wrong with her if she's going to put sugar on her steak.*

I put the sugar on my steak, and he *definitely* thought it was different. He laughed about it and said, "You're crazy." However, I think he was feeling my personality. I also knew he thought I was attractive because, as an entertainer, I had *the* look.

I wore a wig 24/7, my face was always beat to the gods, and I stayed dressed to impress any and everyone. That was all part of the **game**. I enjoyed the mystery of keeping certain things from him, and I planted seeds of deception for entertainment.

A few days later, Jeff said to me, "I don't know how I feel about this. I'm not sure about this guy—this guy who plays *professional basketball*. I'm not feeling this. When he came to get you the other night, he never got out of his car to come to the door. He just sat outside, blowing his horn." Jeff was exasperated. "I'm done with him," he stated. "He sat out there for that long, and he couldn't get his behind out of the car?" (By the way, Jeff is Caucasian and Jewish. Sometimes he had excellent advice, and other times I didn't think so. He was a voice of reason for most of our business decisions and some of our personal ones. Sometimes we listened, but quite often we didn't.) Since Jeff could not understand why Mr. S. hadn't gotten out of his car, he was done with him because of it. In my mind, we were playing a game, so it was all sport.

Although Mr. S. grew up in a Catholic school, he was not a strong spiritually. If I'm honest, I wasn't much stronger than he was. I was aware of the Lord and had just begun seriously abiding in Him. I started teaching Mr. S more about Christ, and his interest grew. He would say, "Okay, I want to know about this Lord, Jesus Christ. I'm feeling you, so I want to know more." He said he wanted to know more about the Lord, but truthfully, he just wanted to learn more about me, which was fine.

Pretty soon, we had begun to see each other every day. Although we had issues with communication, I figured that most relationships had these sorts of problems, especially when they were brand new. I knew he hadn't committed to me, but I fooled myself into believing he was. In my heart, I guess I felt he wouldn't dedicate that kind of time if he wasn't serious about us.

If you've heard of the R&B singer Aaliyah, then you probably remember one of her hit songs entitled, "If Your Girl Only Knew." That song would've made a good theme song for my life because of the sheer arrogance in which I operated. I say this because when I met Mr. S, I learned he was already dating someone. I had a boyfriend I was parting with at the time from back home. Then, Mr. S started to call, visit, take me out for dinner, and do all the other things that go along with dating. To me, all signs pointed to him being serious about me, even though he had not officially broken up with his girlfriend.

Eventually, I decided that I wanted to make sure they were no longer an item, so I started my plan. Now at this time, I was a member of a group called the Sounds of Blackness as a side job, and we got all sorts of gigs performing around town. One of my bandmates was friends with Mr. S's girlfriend at the time.

One day after having rehearsals for a performance, my friend, Bridge, ironically started talking about Mr. S's girlfriend, who I'm going to call Chica. Once I realized they were friends, I started plotting and decided to put a plan in motion to get her down there to meet me.

Chica was gorgeous. I think she was modeling in the city, but I didn't care about that. I was prepared for another game to begin, so I walked backstage to see this lady who had been waiting. Her friend, my bandmate (Bridge), introduced us to each other.

"Hi, how are you?" I asked.

She responded with a little smile, "I'm good, you know. How are you?" Without breaking a sweat or allowing me to respond, Chica continued. "So, I hear you're seeing my boyfriend."

"Who's your boyfriend?" I quizzed before she went on to describe Mr. S to me. "I didn't know he had a girlfriend," I told her when she finished. "We spend a lot of time together, and he's never mentioned anything about a girlfriend."

"You spend time with him?"

Just as I was about to give her an answer, my phone rang. It happened to be Mr. S. "Hey, sweetie, what's going on?" I asked as I picked up the call.

Chica stared at me, and I could almost feel her disbelief as she watched me carry on a conversation with the man she claimed was her boyfriend. A few minutes later, I got off the phone and turned back to her.

"I just would have never known you're seeing him," I stated matter-of-factly.

"I don't even understand this. He's been telling me he just wants to be with me," Chica shared, "and that I'm the only one."

"You know you need to deal with him because he is playing you," I told her. "Like, seriously, you need to deal with him."

A few minutes later, Chica headed home, and I picked up the phone to call Mr. S. I was just playing the game, making sure I'd win.

"How could you have your girlfriend come up to where I'm rehearsing?" I asked angrily. "What kind of lady are you dealing with here?"

"Oh no, I'm not dating anyone," he assured, still trying to get me to go out with him.

Mr. S was upset, and I was utterly evil. I created a plan to play them one against another and sabotage their relationship. I made Chica resent the man she really cared for. I also created the illusion for Mr. S that I was really what he wanted in an effort to get him to remove all distractions, including Chica, and focus solely on me.

In my self-absorbed thinking, I was a celebrity in Minnesota. I was working with the world-renowned Prince. I also sang on projects for Jimmy Jam and Terry Lewis's artist: Low Key (Prof Tee and Lance were big supporters and talented treasures) and Mint Condition (Stokley and his parents were very kind). We were the opening act for various artist, which is how Mr. S met me.

He was a basketball player, and I was a singer, so I felt like it would work for us. He saw me in my world, so some of that was attractive to him. He eventually broke up with Chica as I wanted, and I never thought about consequences since I was still spiritually disconnected. It was all about me getting what I believed I wanted since Mr. S had shown so much interest in me.

By this time, Tam, Vidra, and I had gotten our own place together and no longer lived with Jeff. Mr. S and I started spending more and more time together until basketball season started. He traveled for away games and would tell me, "Hey, I'm gonna be gone. Here's the key; you're welcome to stay at my house while I'm away."

No one had ever said that to me before, and the naïve side of me thought this was the kindest gesture I had ever received from a guy. We hadn't been intimate or anything at this point (although he tried a million times) but having a place where I could go and be by myself sounded pretty cool. He would say, "I'm going to give you the key, so you can come and go as you please." It was nothing but a trick of the enemy.

I was excited that a man wanted me at his place. Learning more about the basketball life and reaping the benefits was just a bonus. He had a great job; he had his own place, and he wanted me to take part in it. He started sharing his life with me. *I must really be amazing to him for him to do all of this* is what I thought. So, I stayed at his house for three or four days while he was gone and packed up to go home every time he returned.

Any time I was gone more than a couple of days, Tam and Vidra would ask where I was. They would tease me and say, "You've been gone a few days. What you been doing?"

One of them mentioned how nice he must be, and everyone kind of minimized me staying over there. I believe because of where we were spiritually (still newbies) no one held me accountable about it or said, "I don't know how smart that is." By then, Jeff felt I was being hardheaded and stubborn and removed himself from the situation altogether. In his words, "She's not listening to me, so I'm taking my hands off of it. That is what she wants to do."

Mr. S and I continued spending more and more time together. Every time he returned from travel, he would come to pick me up and take me out to eat at all these incredible places I had never been to. He was receiving so many wonderful freebies because he played in the NBA. I was just a little "struggling entertainer" who seemingly had blessings on my life. I spent *much time* trying to preserve my image because we were hardly working and had no major income.

Our pay came from the shows we did, or we had little side jobs. We once worked at Fingerhut, an online catalog retailer, four hours a day answering phones. I even sold Kirby vacuums for about three days. I was doing little jobs here and there, and then here comes this man who appears kind and was lavishing me with goodness by taking me out to eat and letting me stay at his place while he was out of town. I was swept away by it all. I was not really talking to anyone who would say it was right or wrong. The conclusion I came up with was that I was feeling him, and he was feeling me.

Soon Mr. S started saying, "Hey, I want you and your girls to have tickets to the games." I started thinking *he's trying to let people see me. He wants everyone to know about us.* I was always feeding myself some vain thought.

Tam, Vidra, and I would get all cute and dressed up to go to his games. We received his VIP treatment. We got to enter through a special entrance, and we had special passes to go behind the scenes where the families and other guests would wait for the players. If you know anything about basketball players, they receive special everything. Their entrances, VIP rooms, and locker rooms are all special. Everything is about them, and the team owners had invested greatly in their players. Their arena was new, modern, and "phenomcellent." My head had grown larger than the moon itself from all of this, being that these were all experiences that were new to me.

Here I was, coming into this basketball world and getting to experience this VIP treatment. I met all the other player's wives and girlfriends. Most of the team players were married, so I went to all of the games and received the same lavish treatment as I connected with these other women.

The basketball wives started pulling me in and telling me, "Hey girl, we need to start hanging together." I was like, "Okay, I'm a basketball girlfriend." I started to think and believe *this is where I'm supposed to be*. However, it was nothing but a mind full of vain tales and foolish thoughts.

Minneapolis was really into its players. Everyone knew their names, and everyone certainly recognized Mr. S. People gave him free stuff every time we went somewhere. Even though all those things were his perks and **ain't nobody know my name**, in my mind, I was the entertainer, and it was about me. All the attention I got made me full of myself to the point where I believed he needed me.

DECEPTION STRATEGY

Mr. S started wanting to spend even more time with me, and because he was very affectionate and always touching me, I said to myself, "I've got to hold out on sleeping with him (having sex) because I know the rest of the girls have given in." And that is exactly what I did. I had planned a defense strategy.

After a while, he asked me to spend the night *with him* at his house. I did, but I wore multiple layers of clothing. My mindset was, *I'm going to stay over here, but I'm locking this sugar cane up*. I was gaming with my guard up. *I'll spend the night, but I must play defense.*

I remember him asking, "Why do you have on all these clothes?" I came up with, "I'm so cold-natured that I have to wear all of this." I don't know what else I said, but at that time, I could come up with excuses in a heartbeat. That went on for months, and he started calling me a "good girl." That was my reputation; he was telling his friends, "She's a good girl," which strictly meant he hadn't gotten the sugar cane he so badly wanted. He was from the east coast, and over there, according to him, east coast guys thought women were either a good girl or a whore. No if's or in-betweens... Good girl or whore. *Period!* Since he couldn't sleep with me, I was a good girl.

CHAPTER 2

Shacking

My father played a huge role in my game plan. He almost walked me through the entire process because he knew this was a professional basketball player I was dealing with. My father was the king of game. He could write an entire book on it.

I shared with my dad, "We've dated each other for a while, and I still don't really know what's going on with our relationship."

My dad was coaching me play-by-play, saying, "Don't stay over there again. Take all the things you might have over there, go home, and don't call him."

I told him, "Okay," and did just that.

Within hours, Mr. S called and said, "I want you to move in. I can't take this. I don't like the fact that your stuff isn't here. You need to come back, and it's time for you to move in."

I told my dad what he'd said, and he responded with, "Yeah, that was the plan. You said you wanted to know where the relationship was. So, you must have a strategic plan to get them to respond. The whole plan was to get your things and leave; don't answer the phone."

He would also tell me, "Okay, now it's time to answer the phone. Answer the phone and see what he says."

"He's talking about wanting me to move in," I reported.

"Well, what do you want to do? Are you ready to move in? How serious do you want to go? Do you see yourself with him?"

All I could say was, "I don't know. I'm still confused."

This basketball life was a whole new challenge for me. I believed my dad had my best interests in mind, but I felt he was also interested in having a basketball player in the family or he had gotten caught up in the challenge of beating this NBA player at his dating game. He was coaching me really on how to get Mr. S to **play the game for life**.

When Mr. S said, "I want you to move in," I had to wrap my mind around what I was going to do, and that turned into, "I'll move in." Just like that, I began packing my things. I knew deep down this would not be a good spiritual decision, but I was so proud he had chosen me.

When I told Tam and Vidra I was moving out of the house to move in with Mr. S, I could tell they had mixed emotions. They stared at me speechless, not knowing what to say. I'm sure they disapproved but felt I probably wouldn't have listened anyway. They were quiet about how they really felt. We were all trying to make it in the music world, so I'm sure they were also trying to have my back and just be supportive.

So I find this law at work: Although I want to do good, evil is right there with me. (Romans 7:21 NIV)

When I moved in, the games went to another level. I now had to create "what do you want him to think about you" scenarios—how I wanted him to perceive me versus the truth. I needed him to believe I could cook; I needed him to believe I could clean; I needed him to believe I could manage a home. There were some parts of those beliefs that were true, but extraordinarily little.

For example, I had never cooked. I had cleaned, but I don't like to. I had also washed clothes and managed a few things. However, I needed him to think I could cook and that I was amazing. So, I started calling my friend in Dallas, Edris, and my mom, asking them for recipes. I cooked up some stuff and had it done by the time he made it in from practice. He was thoroughly impressed.

"Wow! You're amazing. You can cook like this?!"

If you only knew.

No one had taught me anything about this process, so I believed I was supposed to *amaze* him. I started cooking, cleaning, and handling things so well that he started asking me to call his manager and agent to discuss his contracts. That was a big deal—a huge deal—because I was now talking to the person deciding how much money he got paid, where his livelihood would go from there, and how long his contract would last.

At the time, I didn't realize what he was asking of me, nor did I realize how big of a responsibility it was. My interpretation was **he wants me to run things** when I believe he practically only made me a replacement for his mom who was assisting him with most of this. I accepted that responsibility blindly. Again, I knew nothing about what he was asking me to do, but in my mind, I could do it. I was very self-assured about myself and what I thought I was capable of, so I said, "Yes."

Managing so many things became stressful because of the many conversations I needed to have. What I learned was that his mom had been managing everything before I came along, so he had never been responsible for handling anything himself. I did not know that before. What I knew was he played basketball and ultimately shifted her responsibilities over to me.

I'd said yes, not knowing what was demanded or expected of me. I didn't ask any questions. I didn't seek to know what it meant. I didn't understand it either; I only thought this was going to make me look amazing. That's all I cared about—what it made me look like as his girlfriend, and I was still game-playing.

I was still making sure I looked like an incredible character and a wonderful woman who could do all these extraordinary things. That was my goal and my thought process. He needed to see me as astonishing, even though that was not completely the truth.

The basketball contracts started coming. I began having conversations with people who were complaining about certain things Mr. S was doing while playing. I tried to tell him what the agents and coaches were saying, but he made excuses for everything. It got so bad that I even tried to change his thought process.

"They're trying to tell you that you are *not* what they need you to be, and you're saying you're wonderful and great."

By now, we were competing because he was not listening to me. Realistically, we'd been competing from day one. He wanted me to see how *"spectaculous"* and how *"wonderiffic"* he was as an athlete. I tried to let him see how *"fab-mazing"* and *"great-sational"* I was as a person, a vocalist, a manager, and a girlfriend. That went on for a while, and I learned many different things about him I hadn't seen before.

CHAPTER 3

Minimize Red Flags

One day we were watching a basketball game on TV, and one of the players made a three-point basket.

"Wow, that was amazing," I said.

Mr. S replied, "What? You want him or something? You find him attractive? I mean, what's up with that?"

"What are you talking about? I don't even know him; I just said the shot was amazing."

"Is that how you are? You see someone you like, and you just automatically start to go on about them?"

I just got quiet at that point. Who did I just wake up? I had never seen this before. I didn't even know how to respond to it.

After seeing that, it caused me to start looking at other things I might have overlooked. I'd already moved in with him, so I started paying closer attention. I soon noticed that whenever I went to the refrigerator, there was always alcohol in it and on top of it. I couldn't help but wonder why he had so much liquor.

Then, I started noticing he would sometimes be sitting in the den with a glass in the middle of the night. I still didn't make the connection because it didn't seem strange at first. I didn't understand the world of alcohol or alcoholism. I knew of it but had never experienced it firsthand. The way he acted when he had a glass in his hand made me start looking at him differently.

For instance, one night, the girls and I were performing at Glam Slam, in hopes that someone would book us. At that time, Mr. S and I were going to nightclubs with live music quite a bit, so naturally, he was in attendance. Well, Mr. S and I were standing at the bar, and this guy (who was a fan of our singing group) came up to us and said, "What's up y'all?" I turned around and said, "Hey, how you doing?"

As soon as the guy walked away, Mr. S turned around and looked at me.

"I know he didn't just speak to you. I know he didn't. I know you just didn't say something back to him, either."

"Hey, what's wrong with that?"

"Do you want me to call my boys since you and him are disrespecting me right here in front of all these people?"

He was talking loudly now as he held a glass of alcohol in his hand. No one was paying us any attention, but in his mind, I had disrespected him. He was so offended that he felt he needed his boys (who lived out of state, by the way) to handle the guy and to question me **the rest of the night** about my loyalty to him. *What in the world?*

I became silent. I didn't know what to do with that. I was just trying to piece it all together. All I remember thinking was, *I've never met someone who thought like this.* Those attitude changes and outbursts started happening more frequently after he had a glass in his hand. The more comfortable he was with me, the more he drank.

One night, I was at his apartment. After Mr. S returned from going out, he was in the bathroom throwing up. I remember calling my dad saying, "Okay, something is going wrong. He's in the bathroom throwing up and talking crazy."

My dad immediately said, "You know this boy sounds like he drinks too much. You have to tell him you're not having that; you're not putting up with someone who's doing all this drinking."

My dad knew about the other little things that were happening, so I trusted what he said and did exactly as I was told. Whenever I could catch him without a drink in his hand, I would try to talk to him about it. Mr. S would always say, "That ain't no big deal. I can handle my alcohol." He was humble as a dove when he wasn't drinking. He was the quietest, most relaxed person ever until he drank.

I told him that I preferred he didn't drink, and I felt he would comply since he was still trying to figure out how to get me to give up the sugar cane. We were all over each other, yet I was still saying no. I was still playing games. Eventually, he started to drink less, and it made me believe we would be able to move forward from the past.

Misinterpret

I truly believe he had planned to do anything I asked until he got what he wanted. It was part of his process. Since I didn't want him to drink, he devised a plan that would still allow him to indulge in alcohol when I wasn't around. For a period in time, it actually worked.

I didn't see the inquirer anymore. He became very relaxed and started talking about us becoming serious. He started telling me, "You're going to be the mother of my children." In response, I would casually reply, "I am? I'm going to be the mother of your children?"

My interpretation was he wanted me to be his wife. I had convinced myself that he wanted to spend the rest of his life with me. However, all he kept saying was, "You are going to be the mother of my children." (*We as women sometimes don't listen, and we misinterpret.*)

We must listen to what men say. Most men are noticeably clear about what they want. Our interpretation is our interpretation, not theirs. In my mind, he wanted to be my husband because I believed you don't have children out of wedlock.

My upbringing was you don't have kids unless you are married, and if you're talking about having kids with me, then that means you want to spend the rest of your life with me. That's what happens in the world that I grew up in, and I foolishly believed we thought the same way.

Although I would pick and choose what morals I would follow, I kept telling myself he wanted to spend his life with me. However, he simply wanted children with a person he felt would be a good mother—that's all.

At this time, I was speaking to my father about all that had been going on between us. One day I called him and told him I didn't know where me and Mr. S stood.

I said, "Okay, Dad… We've been seeing each other now for like five months, and I'm not sure of exactly what his intentions are."

"You *have* to step your game up and get your answers," he shared.

"What do you mean, Daddy?"

"What does he not like? What does he not like for *you* to do?"

"Well, I don't know what he doesn't like for *me* to do, but what I don't like for him to do is go strip clubs."

Mr. S had a thing about going to strip clubs. He claimed he and the guys just played pool.

My dad asked another question, "So, what are you going to do about that?"

"I don't know." (Like, seriously, what was I supposed to do about that?)

Dad said, "You go to a strip club… Go to a strip club…"

Me, "Okay."

I called my girls and said, "Y'all, we're going to a strip club." It just so happened that some friends I knew were flying in some male strippers from Houston, Texas. They'd posted flyers at the clubs we visited about some men who were supposed to be *fine*. I was telling myself, "This is going to be good." I got hyped up, but remember, I was not where I am now spiritually; therefore, I was straight up going to a strip club!

The plan was in motion. My girls were down for whatever I was down for, so while Mr. S and I were chilling one day, I made sure to say, "We're going to the strip club on Friday," when I was casually getting dressed. "I'm just letting you know," I added.

Mr. S's response? "Oh no, you are *not* going to no strip club."

Why did he tell me that? I told him, "Oh no, you don't tell me where I can't go, especially when you're always just playing pool there. You can't tell me I can't go to a strip club when you practically live at one."

Immediately, he said, "We need to get married!"

Yes, you read that correctly. Marriage was now a discussion. Startled, I questioned, "What are you talking about?"

He reaffirmed his previous statement, "We need to start looking at rings; we need to get married." *What?*

Now every conversation we had before this one, he would always say we needed to wait about three years before getting married. He always told me he wanted to save up more money and to get some more things settled. I'd already told him I wasn't waiting three years for **no one**. I said, "If you come around in three years, and I'm still available, we can see, but I'm not waiting on you for no three years!"

I was dealing with someone not wanting to risk our relationship. I had already said I wasn't waiting for him, and he already felt like I was a good girl. He wanted me to be the mother of his children, and now I was headed to a strip club to watch other men—and he couldn't do a thing about it.

My girls and I went to the strip club and had a blast! I must have been a stripper magnet because those men came and picked up my whole chair with me still sitting in it. They were throwing me up in the air like they just didn't care, and **I loved it!** We laughed hard at the fact that we had not done this before and had so much fun while seeing so many fine, half-naked men! Thank God there were no social media outlets back then.

After I got home, Mr. S watched me get undressed while I happily paraded around the apartment. I could tell he was mad, but he knew he couldn't do anything about it. He was just like, "You can't be serious." I was making all sorts of noises. *You can play pool whenever you want to at the strip club. How 'ya like me now?*

Within an hour of me being home, he said, "I need you to come in here." When I went into his room, he got down on his knees and asked me to join him. He said, "Let's pray; we need to pray."

Now, we weren't very spiritual at the time. We kind of talked about the Lord, but we weren't as serious as we should've been.

Don't Ask Father's Permission

When he said we needed to pray, I quickly knelt to join him. No sooner than I bowed my head, he pulled out a ring and said, "I want you to be my wife. I want you to marry me." I couldn't believe it. He was crying and everything. He repeated it, "I want you to be my wife. I love you. I want to be with you. I want you in my life."

I sat there, taking it all in before I opened my mouth and said, "Yes," and immediately called my dad. "Dad, he just proposed!"

My dad was hesitant, but he said, "Okay." He knew I had put him on speakerphone.

"He just proposed, and I said yes."

My dad was slow to say anything, which was abnormal. His response was more of a calm and dry, "Congratulations…" *Wow.* I knew he was trying to be somewhat happy for me, but he was disappointed that Mr. S had not come to him before asking me to marry him. It was around three in the morning, so I ended the call with, "Well, you know… We love you."

I'll admit Mr. S not getting my father's permission stuck with me our whole marriage. It stayed in the back of my mind all the time because I wanted my dad to have the honor of talking to Mr. S about what this meant and to hear he would be held accountable as my husband.

CHAPTER 4

Prenup for What?

I was engaged, y'all! I immediately went into "Planning a Wedding" mode. *We **must** plan a wedding; it **must** be spectaculous.* We came up with various plans. He started telling his single teammates that we were engaged, and they immediately planted seeds by asking about the prenup. "I know you're not just marrying her without a prenup," I'd heard they'd asked, so then he came home and said we couldn't get married without a prenup.

You know I called my dad, right? He, in turn, told me to say, "If you want a prenup, then you can marry someone else. I don't have time for that."

Ultimately, I told Mr. S I don't do prenups. If he wanted to marry me, there wouldn't be one involved. However, he didn't share the same feelings. He "needed time to think about it."

I personally didn't need a prenup since I believed in marriage and wanted to spend the rest of my life with Mr. S. I'm sure his need for security had something to do with it, but I believed he wanted to be with me too.

When he had decided I was what he wanted, he finally told me, "Okay, all right… We don't need a prenup. Let's just start planning this wedding. Let's get this show on the road."

Disregard His Feelings

As we planned for the wedding, I pretty much had power because he was still trying to figure out how to get intimately acquainted with my sugar cane. Although we set a date in September of 1995, we didn't make it past April without sleeping together. Once we were engaged, I let my guard down. Within months, I found out I was pregnant, and the news completely devastated me. *I can't be pregnant. I can't get married pregnant, and I can't be pregnant. I can't be pregnant. I can't. No, this is not how this is supposed to go.*

Mr. S was happy that I was pregnant because he had it in his mind that he was getting what he wanted. I remember telling him, "We have to get rid of it. I'm not getting married while being pregnant; that's not happening." His reply? "Why? This is what we wanted."

I became another person because I was not taking any responsibility. I had just decided this was not happening; we were not having a baby. That was not the dream I had; it was not the vision. I knew I shouldn't have slept with him but did anyway and look at what happened. I was angry. I allowed my guilt to consume me until I began looking into how much it would cost to have an abortion. The only thing is, I needed to get the money from Mr. S because I couldn't financially do it alone. I could not have a baby out of wedlock.

After arguing back and forth, he finally left the money for me. All he said was, "I have a game out of town. I'm going to leave the money here; do what you've got to do because I'm tired of going back and forth with you on this." It had become the whole relationship. "We've got to get rid of it. We are not doing this," is all I kept telling him.

I walked to the clinic. I don't remember why, but I physically walked about three miles to a facility where they were aborting children. I remember going through the whole process of filling out the paperwork and waiting.

Finally, it was my turn, and they told me I didn't have enough money. *Wow. Not enough money?* I was about $100 short, and I had to go back home and call him.

"I couldn't get it done. They said I need more money."

"Titia, this is a sign. You are supposed to keep it."

I could tell he genuinely wanted the baby, but I kept insisting it was no sign at all; I just needed more money. The next day, I walked back there again with way more money than I needed.

Within hours, I had gone through an abortion. I remember feeling the procedure being done and thinking, *I'm so sorry I have to do this, but I cannot have a child now.*

After getting the abortion, I had to wait for hours in the waiting room because I didn't make arrangements for transportation home and could not tell anyone. *How did I do this? How did I get here?* There was a flood of emotions running through me. I was so good at playing this game with him that I didn't even think about getting **here**. I'd gotten rid of a baby. I was overwhelmed, and I felt very guilty. I believed it was what I needed to do, but I felt guilty about doing it.

I went home and told him, and he was hurt. All he kept saying was, "I can't believe it. I can't believe the baby's gone." Although I felt guilty about what I had done, I was relieved at the same time. I was battling with it. I was concerned about what people were going to think. I was also concerned about the thought of telling my parents.

I felt guilty for a long time. I also noticed Mr. S started to change, too. He became more carefree about stuff. For example, he used to call all the time and check on me, or he would come home at a decent time. Those things started to alter. I knew he loved me, but he was also upset that I had aborted his child.

Finally, with the date set and everything in place for the wedding, we agreed to move to Dallas. He decided he didn't want to live in Minnesota anymore; he wanted to move somewhere warmer.

When Mr. S's NBA contract was ending, he was hoping they would offer him a new deal. I had been talking to his agent (who I thought was giving Mr. S the run around), and he said the coaches had been complaining. I now know that the possibility of his contract ending without the option of re-signing pushed him back toward having a glass a little more frequently. The team hadn't planned to renew his contract or pay him more money, which we were not aware of.

Mr. S was quietly stressing out about his career, which I understood, but I didn't know how to help. When the season was over that year, we moved back to Dallas and stayed with my parents since we had decided to build a house along with planning our wedding.

Before we got married in 1995, it seemed like he was trying to figure out if he could spend his life with me. Mr. S started asking me crazy stuff that didn't make sense.

"If I throw up, would you clean it up?"

I mean, I guess, but probably not. Ha!

"If I was 70 years old and you had to take care of me, and if I couldn't clean myself, would you clean me?"

What are these questions? Why do you keep asking me?

He was trying to see if I was **the one**. We hadn't gone through those things together. He had waited to be intimate with me all that time, and now we were planning a wedding. I believe Mr. S always wondered why he didn't get that prenup. However, regardless of his feelings about the prenup, he decided that marriage was what he wanted to do and something that he was going to do with me.

CHAPTER 5

All About Me

M r. S and I had become so consumed with our own thoughts that we found ourselves lost. We were in the same book but on completely different pages. Because I had not taken his opinions into consideration, our wedding got a tad bit out of control. We'd gotten so lost that even our wedding was a little bit dramatic. It cost about $20,000 and was all about me.

Mr. S would tell me the things he wanted or liked, and I would take them into consideration. I would say, "Oh, okay," and move right on and do whatever I wanted. When he said, "I want to have a nice reception (about 2 weeks before the wedding)," I responded with, "This is what we're going to do. We are *not* going to have a sit-down reception. I plan to have about three or four tables, and everyone's going to stand up and hold their food." That's what I said, and we paid $5,000.00 for it. He was livid.

Mr. S was also upset the week before we got married because there were many issues with the wedding coordinator, who just so happened to be a friend of mine. We believed we had hired someone who misused our money. We paid her, but we did not get all of what we had asked her for. She would say what she couldn't get, or this or that wasn't available, even though we had given her plenty of money for it.

Mr. S admitted that he'd wondered what he was getting himself into. He'd questioned if that was how shady my friends truly were. Slowly but surely, he was starting not to see me as the "good girl" he had once known.

When we got to the wedding and didn't see half of the flowers and décor we had paid at least $10,000 for I was floored. I tried to appear happy, but I couldn't. I knew Mr. S was angry because he couldn't stop wiping sweat off of his forehead. Everyone who knew us could probably tell there was something wrong, even though we tried extremely hard to mask our true feelings.

There were over 1500 people at the wedding. The church was full, and they had to squeeze close together to be seated. We held it at that location because they sat about 1500 individuals, and that's how many people we were expecting. Everybody had RSVP'd. Yet, for all those people, I had only reserved three tables for the reception. I didn't even care who wanted to sit down. You can imagine how upset Mr. S and his family were.

Until that day, I had never been to a reception. I had seen pictures and knew what people said they did at one, but I couldn't remember knowingly going to one. I do know my mom and stepfather got married and had a big party where there was food and fellowship. Still, I had disconnected from it to the point where I couldn't tell you anything about it or what it was. I just wanted to be married. That is what I kept saying, "I just want to be married." I didn't care about the reception. Mr. S, of course, knew about it, so he wanted one. When he didn't get it, he was agitated.

In addition to all that was happening, my younger brother, Lulanger, didn't make it any better. He was a walking production, and that's putting it mildly. If I moved to Minnesota, my brother moved to Minnesota. If I moved back to Dallas, my brother moved back to Dallas. If I was getting married, my brother was moving in with us. That's just how it was, so when it was time to get married, I thought my brother was fine with it.

Lulanger may have seemed fine, but it was like dealing with another bridezilla on my wedding day. "What is wrong with my suit?" he asked. "Do I have a dressing room?" He put on a production about everything, bringing all kinds of drama as if it didn't matter this was my wedding day. "Who's ironing my pants?"

He was so loud. Everyone could hear him coming into the church, talking at the top of his voice. Everyone was asking, "Who is that?" but they knew it was my brother. It got to the point where I had to say, "You all had better get him because if I have to go out there..." The words rolled off my lips and faded mid-air. Someone said, "Titia, you stay over here," because they knew our relationship. I would have whipped him like he was my son.

After showing out for a little while, Lulanger calmed down for a bit. He sang at our wedding and did a beautiful job but later acted out again. I had a hard time with him that day. I do know most people with diabetes can be over the top with their emotions when their sugar is irregular, and my brother was a testament to that.

Whenever Lulanger's sugar fluctuated, his emotions went with it. His behavior was magnified on my wedding day, and because I knew that, I wondered, *Lord, Jesus, what am I dealing with today?* He was putting it on thick, and no one could specifically deal with him. People kept saying, "Okay, you all need to call Titia because we can't deal with him." He was all over the place, and he let everyone have it.

He also made everyone laugh; no one took it *that* seriously, even though they knew he was serious. Everyone just thought it was hilarious because he was overly dramatic everywhere he went. There were too many emotions going on, and I couldn't handle him like I wanted to because I was trying to get married, plus I was thinking about all the stuff going wrong. Even still, with everything that happened, Lulanger was acting a clown, which turned out to be the icing on the cake on *my* day.

At the end of the night, Lulanger ended up being fine and back to his normal dramatic self. I was grateful I didn't have to hurt him because I was tempted. Although we were very close, my brother knew how to set me off. Although he was happy for me and loved Mr. S, he struggled with me not being as available as I had normally been to him.

CHAPTER 6

Vengeance is Mine

Shortly after we got married, while we were still staying with my parents, Mr. S got a call to come to Puerto Rico to play basketball. He didn't know I picked up the phone at the same time he answered and overheard the players telling him that the women were waiting for him to get there and wanted to know when he was coming. The players spoke of how beautiful these women were and how they had plans for him upon his arrival. Mr. S was responding with excitement, saying he couldn't wait to go. Now, you can imagine how upset I was hearing my new husband excited about women in Puerto Rico he hadn't even met yet.

I never told Mr. S I heard his entire conversation, and he had no idea I was on the phone. I wanted to see what he was going to tell me. I remember asking repeatedly when *we* were leaving for Puerto Rico. He gave several excuses as to why I would meet him there weeks after he got a chance to get settled and learn the city.

I expressed to him, "I'm your wife. I want to leave with you, and you're telling me I can't go?" I asked him numerous times to take me with him.

I had absolutely no reason to stay behind. To hear him lie about needing time to get settled caused me to begin to scheme on how I was going to get him. I had surpassed angry. I didn't just want to be an option; I was his wife, for God's sake!

Being Mrs. S had become my entire identity, and he acted like it was nothing. That destroyed me, so I decided to get him back for it. (Now mind you I could have confronted him; I just chose not to. I preferred vengeance.) I knew having an ex-boyfriend around would assist my devious thoughts, so I started talking again with the ex I stopped seeing to date Mr. S. I didn't know what the plan was, but I was open to whatever would cause the most pain because I was that angry. I didn't care about my vows because I didn't even remember what mine were. All I knew was that I was committed to a payback. I replayed his excitement about the women waiting for him over and over again and him telling me I was not coming with him.

I started spending more time with my ex-boyfriend because he fed my flesh with compliments and gave me maximum attention. Each day I became more flattered by my ex's words, but again I also remembered Mr. S's excitement about the women in Puerto Rico and how I was left behind.

I even noticed how he was suddenly a lot less available when he arrived in Puerto Rico. He wasn't answering the phone as often as he used to, and he always claimed he was either asleep or didn't hear the phone ringing, even though I would call throughout the night. All that did was fuel my revenge. I believed Mr. S would regret he had ever gone away without me; that's what kept me going. I was fuelled by getting back at him because of his excitement to be with other women. That was the deception the enemy put in my head. *Yes, yes. Keep thinking that. Keep thinking you're getting back at him.*

Entangled in the excitement of vengeance, I had gotten caught up in knowing I was getting back at Mr. S. After listening and enjoying how I was so meaningful to someone else, everything about this revenge was bringing me joy until… I went as far as to sleep with my ex-boyfriend. Yes, I had physically committed adultery.

At the moment of intercourse, I suddenly realized what I was doing and became overwhelmed with grief. It felt like the visualization of Adam and Eve when they realized they were naked after they disobeyed God. I started crying out loud and asked my ex-boyfriend to leave. I was so upset with myself about what I had done that I never wanted to see my ex-boyfriend again. It was over.

I had gotten so caught up in knowing that I was "getting back at my husband" that I had become blinded to the consequences. That's when the Lord shocked me by saying, "You thought it was going to bring you pleasure; now, you are filled with guilt and shame." See, that's what we do. We put ourselves in a position where we think something is going to bring us some type of reward or joy, and it does just the opposite."

"But a man who commits adultery has no sense, whoever does so destroys himself." (Proverbs 6:32)

When we think of our sins, many of them cause us to wonder why we did this or that or how did we get here. I got there because I didn't realize I was becoming insensitive to the consequences of sin. I believe if I had been much more spiritually connected, then the outcome would have been much different.

Don't Wait

Mr. S changed his mind about waiting three years to marry me once I told him I would not wait three years for him to make me his wife. Maybe he always knew he needed more time to be free and shop some more. He proposed as quickly as he did because he knew early on what he wanted, and that was for me to be the mother of his children. That was his statement for the entire relationship. I was going to be the mother of his children, and that needed to happen because that was all that mattered.

Our marriage was never about me becoming his wife. It was never, "You are the only woman I want to spend my life with." Those were not his statements nor his intentions. What he always said was, "You are going to be the mother of my children," and I interpreted that as *he wants to be with me. He wants to spend his life with me.* He didn't say those exact words before he proposed.

For whatever reason, all Mr. S saw regarding me was a good mother. I don't know where he got that from because I rarely had children around us. We spent a little time with my nephew when we brought him to Minnesota to stay with us, but he was saying that before then. Mr. S had assumed I'd be a great mom from the beginning, so I think the three years he wanted to wait to get married would have given him the time he needed to get all his "singleness" out. He wasn't going to say that to me, but looking back, I think he was trying to tell me, "I need three more years. I'm not ready." But, at the expense of losing the mother of his children, he made the sacrifice.

I also believe Mr. S always regretted not getting the prenuptial agreement because he never believed in forever for us. I'm sure his thoughts of commitment differed from mine, but because I was making everything about what I wanted, there was no room for anything else.

CHAPTER 7

Confession

Despite everything, Mr. S and I kept going. We moved around with basketball from Puerto Rico to Spain to Michigan to South Dakota and finally to France. In 1996, Mr. S was contracted to play overseas ball in France. Like normal, he went over before I would join him to become acclimated with the city (so he would always say) before he would send for me. During my time alone, I spent a lot of time praying and constantly asking the Lord to forgive me for the cheating I had done. One evening I had been reading the Bible, and I believe I heard the Lord say to me, "Tell your husband of your sin, or your marriage will be destroyed." I remember crying and begging the Lord not to make me tell him I had cheated. I knew I had to, although I battled with the how and the when.

Mr. S decided he was ready for me to come to France, and I immediately started to feel the anxiety of seeing him, knowing I had to share a despairing truth. Once I arrived, although I was always excited to see my husband, all I could think about was *how do I tell him? When do I tell him?* We made it to where we would be living, and I met the sweetest surprise. It was a strawberry-colored poodle Mr. S had bought for us, and I fell in love the moment I saw it.

Mr. S enjoyed having a dog around, but this dog captured my heart, and it felt my love because it would not let me put it down. I named him Chyce, and he was just a few weeks old. Chyce was somewhat of a distraction because he required a lot of my time.

Mr. S would go to practice each day, and then one evening after I had been there a few days, he decided he wanted us to listen to marital tapes every night before we would go to bed. I thought it was a little different, but it was quite sweet. The problem was, while these tapes were playing, I kept hearing the Lord remind me to tell him what I had done. (Side note: It was a six-tape series we were listening to.)

Each night we would listen to a tape, and on the final tape, it requested that you renew your vows while repeating after the facilitator...HALT RIGHT THERE! When I heard the facilitator say, "Let's repeat your vows," I immediately started crying and could not stop. I knew I had to tell him what I had done before we went any further.

Mr. S asked me, "Bae, what's wrong?" While crying, I remember saying, "Honey, you know I love you so much, and I need to tell you something." Mr. S kept saying, "What is it? Tell me what's wrong." I kept crying. Then I finally said, "Bae, I'm so sorry that I cheated on you."

Mr. S sat there quiet for a minute, trying to see if he heard me correctly. He then replied, "You did what?" I just kept crying and repeating, "I'm so sorry…please forgive me." He then stood up, grabbed a glass, and threw it at the wall. He yelled, "How could you do this?" I went on to cry for a while, and he just kept looking at me perplexed. We sat up most of the night with him having a million questions, and I shared as much as I could until we were just exhausted, and I fell asleep on the couch with the dog.

When I woke up the next morning, Mr. S was gone to practice. I stayed on the couch all day with the dog feeling terrible because I caused Mr. S so much grief. He came home that evening and was quiet for a bit, and then he said he wanted to talk. He came and sat on the couch and said, "I've thought about it. I want my marriage. I love you, and we need to work through this."

I will admit I was shocked. I was somewhat in disbelief, but Mr. S didn't do a lot of playing, so I believed he meant it, so I just embraced it. We did remain together, and we had some good times, although Mr. S brought up the infidelity sporadically for at least another year or so.

Before our son was born in 1997, it was crazy how we even found out we were pregnant. I had to go to the doctor because something was physically wrong with me. I was sick all the time, and I didn't know why. After the doctor ran tests, he came back in and said something wasn't right, and he needed to bring in my husband.

STD

After waiting for Mr. S to arrive in the examination room, the doctor informed us that not only was I pregnant, but I also had chlamydia. I was asking, "How could this happen?" That is how clueless I was because I kept thinking, *surely not him. How could I have done this?* I immediately started feeling guilty, and I automatically took the blame. I don't know why I did that, but I'm telling you, I didn't even think about the timeframe. I didn't think about how we had already miscarried a child just months ago or anything else. I just kept wondering *how could I have done this.* It never occurred to me that it had been over a year since I had cheated on him, and I had been to the doctor several times since then for regular check-ups. I also couldn't understand why Mr. S wasn't upset with me.

When we got home, he said we needed to talk. *What is he going to do? What is he going to tell me?* He came out and said, "I've been cheating." All I could say was, "What?" He then admitted to cheating with several people and said, "I'm so sorry, but I want to get through this. I want us to get through this."

I became numb. I was still stuck on the fact that I actually thought it was me. Why I thought it was me is unknown, but I should have known it was him. I tried to figure it out and put all the puzzle pieces together, and when he told me it had happened at these times and on these days and with these people, I was speechless. I already knew he had been cheating before he told me, but to hear him admit it was hard to swallow.

"It was nothing. They were just temporary and meant nothing," he spoke as he minimized everything. "I... I want to work this out. You know I don't want this cheating to be a thing with us. Let's talk about anything that needs to be dealt with right now," he pleaded.

I was very lost at that point because I was pregnant. *Pregnant?* I was pregnant, and I had an STD. I was married and pregnant, having our first consented baby, and I had an STD. Now I'm hearing my husband, telling me he's been cheating on me with multiple women, and now he doesn't want this to be a thing with us. How does that happen?

The doctor prescribed some medication and ordered both of us to take it as prescribed. "You're going to have to take this medication," he informed me, "and we pray it doesn't affect the pregnancy. Both of you have to be committed to making sure this gets taken." I hadn't had time to process anything, and I continually wondered *what is going on.* I'd had an abortion and a miscarriage, so I was concerned about what would happen with the baby I was carrying.

I focused on how to keep the baby healthy. In the meantime, I couldn't even deal with Mr. S. I heard him, and I listened to what he'd say, but I just couldn't with him. All I remembered us saying was something about agreeing that we cannot do this again. That was it for us regarding outside relationships. We had both come clean about it. I had already told him about my adultery, and now he is here telling me.

We both knew what the other had done and agreed we absolutely could not do it anymore. That might've been all I said because I knew we had to move on, which was something I would definitely do and certainly say, "I've got to move on from this. It's time to move on. I've got to focus on this pregnancy. I can't even deal with that right now." For him, I'm sure he was good with that.

Now how I handled this IS NOT a recommendation. We should have really talked about it and communicated how we were really feeling and gotten counseling. I didn't treat cheating as a serious matter.

As the pregnancy continued, we grew closer. All we had was each other at this point since family was on the other side of the world and we were in France. Mr. S was with me every step of the way. He was there for every doctor's visit, and we even had fun going to Lamaze classes together. We were almost put out of the group due to our constant laughing at each other. Mr. S was the proudest man in the world when he found out we were having a boy! I was finally going to be the mother of his child.

CHAPTER 8

You Are Not the Priority

L et's talk about the time Mr. S wanted me to have a business, or so I thought. He bought me a salon and a recording studio. The salon had a bill of about $5,000 a month, while the recording studio was in our home. Mr. S spent about $35,000 to fill the recording studio with music equipment I didn't even know how to turn on because he knew that's what I wanted to do, and I believe he thought it would occupy me. Mr. S was also very supportive of me singing or making music. When he asked what I wanted to do, I answered, "Well, I definitely want to sing and make music." So, he got me a studio.

Back when I was in high school, I became friends with Kirk Franklin and Carnell Murrell. These two (at the time) were up and coming professional Gospel recording artists. Kirk was a choir director and musician known in Dallas and Fort Worth, Texas for his high-energy performances and dramatic conducting. He was crazy-talented and always put on a show, leaving you inspired and invigorated. Carnell's vocal ability and writing skills were out of this world. He had written and produced for I don't know how many artists. These were the first two people I thought to share my studio with because I knew they would appreciate it. They hadn't become household names yet. They weren't well-known as they are now by any means, yet I considered them to be my big brothers.

I met Corey, our engineer, in the studio. He was introduced to me by Carnell. When Carnell found out I had studio equipment, he made our home his home. Because Mr. S was always out of town, it worked out perfectly. Plus, Mr. S knew Carnell respected and loved him dearly. Carnell was married to my dear friend, Ptosha, and they had a family, so all of them would come over. We were all having a blast producing music.

I was the first woman in Dallas, Texas to own and run a top-of-the-line music recording studio in my home amongst my circle of friends. At the time, Pro Tools (industry-standard software makers) was just coming out with all these big technological devices you could use to record. When everyone Carnell and I knew heard I had a studio, they all started coming to my home, and I wouldn't ask them for anything. I didn't ask people to pay me because I didn't care about the money; it was all about making music. *So here I go again, going against my husband when he wanted the studio to make money as well as make music.*

We had people like Isaac Carree (Men of Standard), the former Chris Simpson, Shaun Martin, Bobby Sparks, King Logan, Candy West, Paco, and Rico (another engineer) come over to our home and create music. Earnest Pugh wasn't even a signed artist yet, but he recorded his first project in our studio. We always had someone recording at our house, and no one else had all the equipment I had.

When Bobby Sparks first saw my drum machine, he said, "I really want one of these." It was exhilarating, but I didn't even know what I had. I simply responded, "Oh, okay." He was so excited that he started itemizing. "This cable, right here... Do you know how much this cable costs?" I said, "Yeah," but in my mind, it wasn't a big deal.

Our house was full of people all the time, and I loved it. I *loved* it. It took me back to my childhood with me and my brother longing for people to come over. I *longed* for some company. That was another reason so many people lived with us. In some way, I felt lonely because my husband wasn't always around. That became a whole other challenge in the relationship.

I had lots of siblings who lived in Wichita Falls, Texas. They had never been able to spend the night with me before I married Mr. S, so for them to stay over was exciting for me. I was like, "Oh, my God! I can have my siblings stay with me! They can spend the night. *Wonderful!*" Even today, I love having gatherings; however, I don't necessarily need to have people live with me anymore. I'm past that, but I love it when many people come together and have fun or talk and fellowship. I enjoy that *very* much.

Anyway, we had the studio, and all those people were coming in using it. It got to the point where Mr. S would call and say, "You know, it's one o'clock in the morning. Your friends are still at the house." I told him we were just recording, but then he started saying stuff like, "I'm not feeling this." I'd try and convince him this was a good thing. They were teaching me music. **I was learning how to use the machines.**

You must remember, when you have a motive, you're not thinking about the consequences. That's been my whole message with this book. We make decisions, but we don't know the outcome. For instance, I taught Mr. S to play Dominoes, and that backfired on me. His motives were to keep me occupied, but he didn't like me having other priorities.

It appears Mr. S thought me having my own studio would be a good move, so to speak, until it didn't work in his favor. Almost as if me doing something I enjoyed would keep me from distracting him while he played Dominoes or video games. I guess he figured I wouldn't be paying as much attention to him or needing him by being at home 'occupied,' but no. He didn't like that because there were more men at our house than women. To the guys, the studio was a big toy store. It was like they came over to play. Do you know how crazy that was? Well, they did; all the time, to the point where whenever Mr. S called, he would ask, "Who was that?"

At the time, many of those friendships were new to me. I knew of some of them but hadn't spent much time with them. Having a studio allowed me to create bonds with people that are still strong to this day. Many of them I can call now, and they'll ask, "Girl, do you remember what you did? Yeah, I got you." I believe they all felt like I encouraged them to win on some level.

I didn't know if I was helping them. I just felt like fellow artists should come over. You know, in my mind, I wasn't thinking about the long-term musical aspects of it, and I didn't know back then that helping would be called career-building today. I was just thinking, *they're coming over!* That was the thing for me. Having people around was my drug.

Take the Relationship for Granted

At some point, Mr. S's concern led to even more phone calls. "Who's over there now? What are you all doing?" I would get calls every hour, to the point where I started telling him, "Okay, you are straight *wearing me out.*" (This is me talking now, though, being ignorant.) I reiterate, "You are straight *bugging me.* Like, why are you calling so much?" I wasn't getting the attention the way I wanted it, so I wasn't feeling any of his calls and he was regularly frustrated that someone was in the studio.

I remember some of my friends also came over because I was doing hair at that time. Even though I had a salon, I never really went much because people preferred to come to my house. When Mr. S would call, sometimes I'd be like, "Oh, I have a client under the dryer." There was always something as to where I started to feel like he was bothering me.

One night Mr. S called while away playing basketball, and I think he had been drinking because he was talking *really* crazy. He kept hanging up on me and calling me right back—literally. I asked him, "*Now* what are you doing? Didn't you *just* hang up on me?" He didn't want to hear what I had to say. *Click.* Then he called back, and I answered, "Well, hello." He would ask, "So, who's over there with you?" Whether he liked it or not, I retaliated and hung up because I knew he wasn't even going to remember that conversation the next day, which he didn't. One night I told him, "You are *so* insecure." That was one of the worst things I could have ever said to him. Something flipped for him when I said that. He responded, "Oh, you think I'm insecure? Okay."

He hung the phone up, and from that point on, he never questioned me about anything else. In fact, he never *cared* about one more thing. Mr. S *totally* shut down. *Totally*. Something went off in his head to where I guess he figured, *well, that's it. I'm not asking you about another thing. I don't care what you do.* He didn't say that, but that was how the rest of our marriage felt.

I could come in when I liked, and sometimes I would do stuff on purpose to see if he was going to respond. He never said a word. The stuff I knew bothered him in the beginning, like being on the phone with another man who might've been coming over, did not get a response. I could come home at five or six in the morning, and he would not say anything. I started wondering if something was wrong with him, but I hadn't made the connection right away.

I never considered that last phone call, so I didn't get it right then. Then one day, as I started playing back the videos in my head, I had a *no; you did that* thought. *You told him he was insecure, and you said it in such a way that he felt emasculated.* (I know me: if I said it like I thought I said it, then he was bleeding.) *Know what I'm saying?* Like, there was blood somewhere because that's how I communicated. Mr. S used to say this to me, and it was a term he used quite often, "You are killing me softly. You are killing me softly."

CHAPTER 9

Accusations

A year or so had passed, and Mr. S was now playing basketball in the CBA (Continental Basketball Association) again and asked me to visit him on a road trip to Indiana. The following is what alcohol contributed.

I get settled in the hotel room waiting for Mr. S to arrive from practice and then decide I need to go to the payphone in the hallway to call and let my dad know I had arrived since he was keeping our son, G2, while I was traveling.

"Who were you talking to?" he asked with a sneer on his face.

"I called my dad to check on our son," I replied.

"So, you mean to tell me you've been talking on the phone to your dad? You want me to believe that? You expect me to believe you were out there talking to your dad?" he asked angrily. "My teammates walked by just now. They told me you were on the phone. Who were you talking to?" he repeated, this time his voice going up a notch.

At this point, I just started laughing. I laughed because I was in disbelief that this appeared to be a tantrum about me calling my dad. To me, this was plain funny. Suddenly, he grabbed me and started shaking me, and then threw me down to the ground with a more menacing voice and repeated, "I said, 'who were you talking to?'"

That had never happened before. He had never caused me to be fearful of him ever. All I remember doing was grabbing all my things. I didn't even bother to listen to him anymore. I hadn't dealt with that kind of behavior, and I wasn't about to figure it out. I'd never had to deal with an abusive relationship or anything physical, so that reaction was new to me. Although I'd heard him say ignorant things, Mr. S had never touched or put hands on me, but that day he literally grabbed and threw me and was very livid. I think my laughter set him off.

When he did that, I *immediately* got what I could and went to the front desk. I was frantic and began to plead with the attendant, "Sir, I don't know how this works, or how this needs to happen, but I need another room. I cannot be in the room with him." The attendant immediately jumped into action and got me another room and key. He could tell something was wrong.

I went back to get the rest of my things, and luckily, I hadn't unpacked yet, so I just grabbed what was left and walked to the other room. Of course, Mr. S yelled at me, asking where I was going, but I ignored him. I couldn't care less about anything he said at that point.

As soon as I got to the new room, I took a minute to pray. All I could say was, "Lord, what have I done? What is going on? How do I handle this? I'm clueless about what to do." It was a cry for help from me because I seriously had no idea what I was supposed to do next.

Mr. S kept coming over all night and knocking on the door, but I wouldn't answer. Finally, at around 5:00 AM, he slipped a note under my door. It was a two-page letter saying how sorry he was and how he would stop drinking because he knew what he had done was wrong. I still was unsure of how to respond, so I let him in after about an hour and decided to hear him out.

He kept apologizing and telling me how he was going to change. He realized he had made a mistake and admitted the alcohol had played a role in how he'd responded. We sat and talked most of that morning, and then I decided to go to bed. We had talked so much, and I had been up all night listening to him bang on the door, so I was worn out. I fell asleep, and when I woke up later that morning, we did talk a little more. It was very intense and very emotional for me and for him.

However You Go in Usually Remains

Whatever negatives you deal with dating usually get worse when married. Most of the people I knew who had gotten married at the same time were learning, too. None of us had another couple pouring into us. It would have made a difference. In fact, the Bible speaks about the necessity of older women teaching younger women. That's why I'm praying this book will cause someone who may not even know they need to be taught or even want to learn to realize they have choices and that these choices have consequences. Through this book, I'm showing all the different scenarios of my foolishness and ignorance to teach the after-effects of doing things our own way.

Even through all of our issues, in just less than two years, we found ourselves expecting yet another child and we were both excited. After we had our son, we knew we wanted to go ahead and have another one right away since children were what he wanted. I became very nauseated, and the scent of my husband was literally making me sick, especially certain soaps he used. I later found out I would have to go through most of this pregnancy while on bed rest.

Labor Pains

Before I had the baby, people told me I was emotionally all over the place—and I was. The night I went into labor, Shanika (my dear friend who was a Godsend) spent the night with me because my water could break at any moment, and I was home alone. Mr. S was away playing basketball, and my son was with his grandparents. I remember getting up to go to the bathroom and saying, "Our house is flooding! Why is there water everywhere?" It was my water breaking!

Shanika called my mom, and she came immediately. We jumped into the car, and the contractions were killing me, but between them, I asked for the eyebrow pencil because my eyebrows needed doing for this delivery. *Let's not forget, I was still quite vain, so I was very mindful of what I thought my appearance should be for others.* When we headed to the hospital, I called Mr.

S and said, "Get on a plane! The baby is coming!" I then made up my face, so I would have good pictures.

I had a little time in the room to wait before the pushing would begin. Shanika and my mom were there waiting with me. I was in labor for about two hours. My sister, Tweety, arrived and stayed with me during the entire birthing process. I'm very grateful she was there.

I knew I wanted a girl, but I did not want to know beforehand what I was having. We purposely found out for Mr. S during our first pregnancy because he had already said, "I want a boy first. I want a boy first," so I said, "Lord, give him what he wants. I don't care at this point," the first time. (One of the times I wasn't selfish.) However, with the second child, I wanted a girl. That's all I kept saying. So, when we had our big boy, G2, I was fine with knowing, but for Elizabeth, I preferred not to know.

I successfully delivered a beautiful and healthy baby girl. Elizabeth (my butterfly) had arrived! Her dad came in literally two hours later. From the time I got off the phone with him until he arrived, he'd been on the way. The basketball association had airplanes for the coaches, players, etc. in case of emergencies, so once he found out I had gone into labor, he got onto one of the planes and walked into the hospital hours later. I was disappointed he missed the birth, but happy at the same time to see him.

Mr. S took Elizabeth from me and held her close in his arms, and I thought, *oh, my God, I've got some help.* I was so happy. I felt like I had some relief, even if just for that short while. We had a hospital room full of people—family and friends alike. Tam, Isaac, King David, Peaches (Peacha), Candy, Jada, Talisha, Shanika, Tweety, my mom, and others were there for support. They were trying to figure out who each other was. Everyone just wanted to see and meet Elizabeth because this was our first girl. I was thinking, *I'm so glad I did my make-up.*

Soon after Elizabeth was born, the basketball season was ending, and Mr. S had not received a new contract to play. He decided to start working at an elite car dealership to provide income. Over time, as he worked there, different occurrences started happening. Things began to change quite a bit.

CHAPTER 10

Neglect

I became frustrated because I noticed more and more that Mr. S was doing less and less. He was doing nothing but having fun. I looked at the house getting dirty, and all of the other responsibilities being neglected, and I tried not to be stressed. I think that was why the bed rest was so important. My body had gone through a lot, and I mentally broke down about the house.

First, there was so much house. Secondly, although I didn't like to clean, I didn't like things not being tidy or kept together, but due to my sickness and being told by doctors to stay in bed, it wasn't easy for me to watch my home out of order under the circumstances. Mr. S was not willing to do any cleaning.

Now, keep in mind, before having the baby—probably the last few months before her birth—I was home alone on bed rest by myself. All these thoughts were going through my mind like *see, he ain't never here. I'm just going to do this stuff by myself.* Mentally, I truly was all over the place because I was dealing with the stresses of life, like "married while single parenting," managing the home alone, and being concerned about my husband's whereabouts.

I started to realize that before being married, I had never lived by myself. I went from home, to college, then to Minnesota with Tam and Vidra to a husband and then a family. When he wasn't there or when other people weren't around, I would wonder where everyone was. That was torture for me. I didn't like being alone at all, so the thought of him not being there bothered me even more. *That was something new I was learning about myself but had not learned how to communicate it at that point.*

Once we were released from the hospital and had gotten settled in at home, I was hoping the four of us would start to develop a much closer bond. While bonding with children and my family came naturally for me, I felt like I needed to nudge Mr. S to show that he could connect with the rest of my family and bond with them too. One way for us to do that with my family was to play Dominoes together. I never played often, but I knew how to. Thus, I told him, "I'll teach you how to play Dominoes, so you'll know how when you're around my family."

That was the worst thing I could have done. Mr. S was addicted to competition to the extent that if you came to our house in the evening and you were going to play Dominoes, you would not leave until maybe 6:00 or 7:00 AM. He was committed to making sure he didn't just win, but that he skunked you wearing stank by the time you left. He was *that* serious about it, and my current stepfather enjoyed it too. Mr. S would sometimes go to my parent's house, and he wouldn't come home until the next day. That was outside of the 70-80% of the year he spent traveling!

My stepfather wasn't thinking that Mr. S had not spent time with his family even when he had just gotten back into town. He would just tell us, "He likes playing Dominoes, so he can stay over here as long as he wants to." That was a problem for me because we had a new baby. I was trying to make Mr. S understand that his wife and child were his priority; however, he received it as me trying to control him.

Looking back, I wasn't very transparent with anyone other than my father. I mean, I talked to my dad a whole lot, but very few others at this point. Dad called me regularly then. Now what I did realize, after the fact, was that he started showing his hand about how he really felt.

When I would call to talk to my dad about life after marriage, he would talk to me for about a minute or two, and then he would say, "Hold on. Let me put your stepmother on the phone." In other words, he was saying he'd gotten me married, but I'd have to figure the relationship out. Yet, at the same time, I learned years later he knew it wouldn't last.

I had followed everything my dad had said, so I still asked, "What do I do next?" I relied on him because Mr. S was a serious relationship that I'd brought him into, and I felt I needed a man's perspective. I valued everything my dad said, and I looked at it as him guiding me because he knew the game so well. It was me simply saying, "Okay, this is a new relationship, and I don't know what I'm supposed to be doing. I don't want to make mistakes. So, can you help me?" And, if that meant playing the game, okay, I played a game. I didn't know any better, so I did it. That's just how it was.

Dad was my coach; we talked all the time. I adored him, but he hadn't necessarily poured into me about me as an individual. He poured into me about his life and what his experiences were, like the things he was able to get away with—*from a man's perspective* or the lessons he had learned. However, that wasn't necessarily teaching me all I needed to know. I was lacking integrity, character, and honesty as a wife. I had magnified the negative, and that altered who I was. I had allowed my dad to shape my thoughts based on his past ways. As I said earlier, you're training a child whether you realize it or not, and from that it taught me to always pray with my children and really listen to them.

Confession: I was never really into the guy I cheated with romantically. He had helped me in the beginning when I needed him, which is why I could call him and know he was going to be there. He really was a friend first. For instance, he would encourage me to talk about things going on with me, whether it was positive or not. I thought something was wrong with me opening up or expressing myself, and my ex-boyfriend assured me it was okay to be transparent. When I finally did, I remember I would just cry while getting it out because I had never shared my emotions before. It was painful to reach inside myself and tell someone how I truly felt about anything—to say I don't like this, that, or something altogether. This ex-boyfriend allowed me to do that.

I became more comfortable with sharing when we were talking because I started telling myself, "You know, you don't get to talk. You don't." It wasn't always so much that someone told me I couldn't talk; it was just that no one was ever around to talk to or listen. My mom worked; she traveled regularly. When she was home on the weekends she rested, or we visited our cousins. I did more listening on the phone to my dad than I did talking to him growing up.

My brother, Lulanger, was younger than I was, so we weren't having serious conversations as kids. We were having "Are we going skating this weekend?" conversations. So, I didn't have to get deep or respond to, "Hey, how 'ya feeling?" Our conversations were always, "You need medicine," or "Have you eaten?" They were not, "What does this or that feel like?" or "How do you express yourself in a relationship?" Those conversations didn't start happening until we became adults; by then, I was free. I mean, I cared about other people, and I still do. You just weren't about to get my feelings out of me.

My first boyfriend in high school, Mac, used to say, "Please, talk to me. Please, tell me how you feel." I would say, "I can't." He would want to know if I was upset about something or not, and I couldn't—or simply chose not to—communicate. Although I would not always share with him, I did care about him deeply and wanted him to be in my life, yet I was so immature.

In all of this, I found out we look for a man to complete us when we really need to know ourselves and who we are in the Lord. This can take a long time to realize. Many times, we don't know yet that we don't know who we are, so we end up connecting with anyone we think loves or likes us.

CHAPTER 11

Church?

Something else we had issues with was that there were things I thought we needed, but he didn't. When we first came to Dallas, we found a church home at Tabernacle church; we were there for about a year. Well, he decided he didn't want us there anymore. I told him, "Fine, let's go look for another church."

Mr. S wanted to go to my stepfather's church, I didn't. Eventually, we decided to start visiting Oak Cliff Bible Fellowship (OCBF) Church, and we both really enjoyed it. Here's the thing, though. In hindsight, I think because Mr. S was spending so much time with my stepfather playing Dominoes and hanging out that they were bonding, and I believe that's what was causing Mr. S to want to attend his church.

When we attended my current stepfather's church as teenagers, my brother would be back there, clowning and joking, and entertaining with the girls on one side of the church while I was over on my side in another world. I heard the Word, but my understanding of it was bad. I needed elementary teaching. Most of the time, there was a distant connection to what was going on unless I was singing or part of the young women's group. We lived at church; I just wasn't allowing the Word to live in me.

When I moved to Minnesota, I was 22 years old. I hadn't planned to return home. Once I settled in Minnesota, I started going to New Salem. I believe that was the first time I sought out a church of my own.

When Mr. S and I were looking for a church in Dallas, like I said, we visited and enjoyed Oak Cliff Bible Fellowship. We liked our former church, which was Tabernacle, but we started feeling like we were favored because of Mr. S's status. The pastor would even call Mr. S out sometimes to be prayed for, talking about being blessed financially and how he could be a blessing to the church.

Mr. S wasn't necessarily knowledgeable about the Lord's word, but he could certainly feel when something was wrong, and he knew for sure this was a 'something ain't right' situation. He was correct. Even what I saw made me think *this is crazy... why is he picking us out of everyone in this church and dealing with money. Why is he having him commit to giving?* That's why we left. Mr. S said, "We're not coming back here. We're *not* coming back here." I was fine with it because after the pastor did that one last time, I definitely had enough of it.

Anyway, we started going to Oak Cliff regularly. I really, *really* liked it. He really, really liked it as well, it seemed. Mr. S had decided for us that he wanted to go to another church, which was my stepfather's, and I disagreed with that. Whenever I opposed something, that's when I felt like, *okay, now I gotta get my daddy involved because he's going to tell me how to handle this.* That's what I'd always gone to him for, and this was no different.

I called my dad and said, "Dad, Mr. S wants to leave and go to our old church." He didn't have a whole lot to say about it. He simply replied, "Let me let you talk to my wife." He then put my stepmother on the phone, so I talked to her about it. She recommended, "Just make sure that whatever church you attend has a strong teaching with strong Christian principles. So, if you prefer to go to Oak Cliff, you will need to stand firm." After hearing what she said, I knew I had to strongly convey my direction on the matter. Well, I took that and put hot sauce on it. Then, I added layers with my own style of communication.

One Sunday, we were getting ready for church, and I asked, "So, we're going to Oak Cliff, right?" He was like, "No, we're going to go to your stepfather's church." I was adamant. "No! We're not. We are *not* going there." He wanted to know what I was talking about, so I told him. "First of all, I've done some research and Oak Cliff has spiritual growth classes we can connect with, and if we're going to grow spiritually, then I want us to connect with others dealing with families and children. Secondly, I grew up in my stepdad's church and now prefer to venture out and go somewhere else. I prefer to go to Oak Cliff," I stated.

I went on this whole tirade, and he stood there looking at me like he thought, at that moment, *I don't even know what to do with you. I won't fight with you because you're just too much.* Still, he didn't understand why I came at him like that. There were times when I might have disagreed a little bit; then there were other times where my stance was enormous. That one was "really big."

I believed if we went to my stepfather's church, my husband would be focused on competition and Dominoes more than a closer walk with the Lord. For Mr. S, it was just that he wanted us to go there—I believed so they could hang out more. I put my foot down. "No, we are *not* going there." I refused to listen to any of his thoughts on the matter. I was stubborn as a mule and would not listen to any thoughts that disagreed with mine.

That was me not praying about anything; simply taking matters into my own hands. I never even asked him the reason he wanted to attend; I just assumed.

Mr. S decided to attend Oak Cliff Bible Fellowship with me. He appeared to be ok with it, but it was obvious that it wasn't what he wanted to do—almost like he dreaded it. Not because he wasn't enjoying the service, but because I was calling the shots. Truthfully, I didn't see this as I was running something; I just felt I was standing firm on my desire. We were functioning in a marriage in a way God did not intend. I surely wasn't praying and trusting the Lord regarding Mr. S's desire.

Once it all came tumbling down, I'm telling you with the help of DeAnna Brown (who later became my mentor), I went through every Free At Last counseling class at OCBF I could find to help me figure me out. I was very lost, and I was trying to get the answers from anyone who would give me the time of day because I was still growing in the Lord.

Remember, years earlier, when I lived in Minnesota, I was going to church, but we were singing R&B. We went to church because we knew we were supposed to, yet there was no accountability. Sermons were taught, but I can't say they were sermons that were effectively dealing with my walk or convicting me to walk differently in the beginning. Leaving church after Sunday service just felt like, *oh, that was good.* We were going to the club that night because that was the life we were living.

Rhythm & Blues music was our lives back then; I was growing spiritually at a ridiculously slow pace. We focused our attention on how to get a record deal and how to get in front of the next big artists so they could see us. That was my world. I was merely going to church, but when I came to Dallas, I felt like, *okay, I need to seriously get closer to the Lord.* I was desiring understanding, yet I was confused. Like I said, in my mind, I thought I was doing what was right by taking my father's direction. I believed it was the best direction for the relationship; it was really just his experience. I was also foolish in not knowing what the dating process was in reality—even though the instructions were told to me by father, it wasn't divine direction.

In hindsight, after we were married, I would only talk to my dad and stepmom after things had happened. If she said, "Don't say anything to Mr. S," then I wouldn't say anything. I'd let that go on for months, and then I'd finally call back and go, "Okay, so that ain't working." By that time, I'd done so much damage, there would be a new thing to call about. I wasn't even phoning about the previous issue anymore. I was constantly trying to get direction; I just wasn't doing it right.

Mr. S would tell me I treated my friends better than I treated him because he could hear me talking on the phone to them. He felt I was sensitive and caring to them. When he would come home and try to act as if everything were okay, something would cause him to throw out comments like this instead having a conversation with me. However, life wasn't exactly *okay* because we each had different issues that we weren't properly dealing with.

For instance, when he played basketball, there was always someone to make sure every hotel he stayed at—even when he had an apartment—got cleaned. Therefore, for him, that should've been happening at home. He figured he made enough money to where his house should be getting cleaned regularly. He did not understand why we didn't have service for everything or why I wasn't doing it all. "Why aren't my clothes getting picked up? Why aren't my clothes getting washed? Why isn't his house being cleaned? Why isn't the trash being taken out?" he'd ask. I was always looking at him asking, "Why aren't you helping with any of these things?"

At times we would try to be together or work together, so to speak, or try to connect, but it didn't happen as much as I would've liked. I had this thing about time; I was clear that was my love language. "I *want* your time. I want *your* time." He wanted some of my time, but he also liked affection. He would enjoy my hand touching his hand, or he enjoyed touching my cheeks, even if for only a few minutes. He was all about some type of touch, and I knew that.

Although we did enjoy one another, we didn't ever seem to be at a good place long. It became a game of who is going to out *not*-love the other most. He felt disrespected. I felt unheard. He felt like he gave up everything for me; I felt like I gave up just as much. We both felt disregarded in the marriage, so it became a relationship competition. Everything was a competition, and that became the conversation. "Do you know what I gave up for you? Do you realize I was a professional basketball player?" he asked. "Well, do you realize I was performing with Prince? Do you realize I was opening for Mint Condition?" I countered, always throwing names.

We had an enormously hard time connecting by that point. He was in and out of town, and when he was home, we always had a house full of people, even for him. Because he now played Dominoes and video games, there were just as many people over with him, and because we had a game room upstairs, he could be up there forever and a day. I was downstairs doing my thing or in the studio, which was down the hall, but we always had something going on because the house was big enough. We could each be somewhere else doing something different, and both be fine with that. Even with all of this roller coaster ride of a relationship we could somehow overlook our differences when it came to intimacy.

Outsiders

Let me remind you we now have a new daughter and a very young son, and I noticed more and more that Mr. S started coming in even later from the dealership, spending less and less time at home. Macon, who would come and record at the studio, and would come over when Mr. S was in town, became his good friend and they started spending time together. They would be in the game room, and then they would leave to play Dominoes. It was almost as if a pre-party was happening in our house, and then those two would figure out how to find an after-party elsewhere. By then, I felt like Mr. S ignored the children and me.

At this point, Mr. S started coming home even later than normal. He and Macon started spending additional time together, but there was something that stood out to me about this particular friend. Macon was my friend first, and there was something that made me uncomfortable about him when he and Mr. S started connecting. When people would come over, they would be there for hours. Sometimes I would fix food or snacks, especially if I knew they were going to be there all night or seemingly until forever. I'd bring out something like tacos, pork chops, or anything else that was quick. I thoroughly enjoyed entertaining; however, I also wanted our guests to leave when Mr. S was home so he could share in the family responsibilities.

Our guests knew I would take snacks upstairs to the game room, so some of our guests were there for the hospitality. I found out later many of them didn't have someone who checked on or served them, but in my mind, I figured they were in my home all that time, and I knew they hadn't eaten, so I took them food. There was one friend of ours who admired that. I just didn't realize how much at the time. However, Mr. S's new friend, my old friend, I'm telling you, I was now uncomfortable with.

CHAPTER 12

If You Seek, You Will Find

As Mr. S continued to come home at different times of the night, Macon continued to visit the studio and have more conversations with me. I soon realized it was more than likely because he had an underlying desire to get to know me personally. I decided to use that opportunity to see if Mr. S still cared. I didn't tell him who it was, but I asked him candidly one day, "You know one of your friends is trying to get to know me?"

At that part of the marriage, he was acting as if he didn't care about me, and I was trying to see if anything mattered to him. He looked at me and asked, "Who? Which one of my friends is trying to talk to you?" The first thought in my mind was at least I got a reaction from him, as I was totally in the clouds about where we were by this point. He was upset about what I'd told him for about five minutes, and then he zoned out. A few days later, Macon came back to me, asking, "Did you say something to him about me liking you?" I told him, "I didn't say you, particularly. I just said one of your friends. I didn't tell him who it was."

Mr. S knew it was one of his closest friends, but I still didn't let him know which one because I needed Macon to keep me updated, which he did. Every time something was going down, Macon would call me and say, "Hey, we're supposed to be going to the pool hall tonight. I'll call and let you know what's going on."

When Macon first started checking on me with, "Hey, you alright?" or "What's going on with you? How's everything?" I simply responded with, "I'm good," but I felt something was up because he was one of the people at the house all the time. I was thinking, *why are you asking me like you're not always over here. You practically live here—with Mr. S.*

He started to call and check on me more frequently to see how I was. Then one day, he randomly asked, "Is anything different with you guys?" I wanted to know what he meant and asked him, point-blank, "What do you mean?" That's when he became a little more specific. "Are you two talking?" he inquired. "You spending time together?" I told him there were some differences and challenges we were facing, but I really couldn't speak to that and didn't really know what he was asking.

Macon asked me if I'd noticed Mr. S had been coming home later. Of course, I'd noticed. I just hadn't said anything, so I told him, "Yeah." Now I'm thinking, *why is he asking me all of these questions.* To my surprise, he informed me that he knew where Mr. S had been going, so I asked him where. He seemed eager to share and admitted Mr. S had been going to the pool hall but was meeting someone. I casually asked him, "Someone like who?" to find out what he knew.

Macon told me there was a young lady Mr. S had been seeing at the pool hall and let me know he'd tried to talk to him to keep him from doing it, but Mr. S wasn't listening. At that moment, I decided I needed to stay connected to Macon because I needed him to give me more information.

What did I do? I started calling Macon with, "Hey, how are you doing? What's going on? What are you all doing tonight?"

Mr. S would go to the pool hall as planned and meet his girl there, and then Macon would call me. "She just got here. They're over there talking," he'd say. Sometimes, he would even tell me when they were leaving. Mr. S would usually leave with her around 3:00 AM, but he still didn't come home. This friend, Macon, was telling me everything, and it was literally tearing me up, yet I wanted to know every detail. I felt helpless.

Macon and Mr. S. had become "tight" friends and were spending more and more time together. I noticed Mr. S continued to come home even later than before. I still said nothing because I got stuck on, "You don't say anything; just pray for him," from the wisdom I had received earlier from my stepmother. Even though I thought there was something wrong with that alone, I was literal with my directions. "Don't say anything," meant don't say anything. Right?

Well, sometimes it would be three o'clock in the morning, then four o'clock in the morning, and then six o'clock in the morning. I finally figured maybe I should just do something instead of saying something. So, what did I do? I decided to come home at five in the morning to see what would happen one night while Mr. S was home with the kids. Absolutely nothing happened—no reaction, no questions, no nothing. Again, in my mind, me not saying or doing anything doesn't feel right, but "be quiet" was all I heard when I had asked what to do.

I tried to stay ahead of whatever was happening, and the more I talked to Macon, the more information he gave me. By that time, my cousin, Sherry, was staying with us. After obtaining more information, she was the one who had helped me in this process. It all started becoming clearer as I talked to her because I would share with her what Macon was sharing with me.

"Okay, my source said Mr. S isn't coming home because he's going to the pool hall, meeting this girl," I repeated.

My cousin said, "Find out her name."

I got to work on doing just that. First, I needed to figure out how to do it, though. I decided to talk to Macon again. I don't know what I said, but I kept reeling him in and finally got him to give me a name. Come to find out…the woman was the sister of someone they were playing basketball with that he'd gotten connected to. I told my cousin—and this is why the world is so small.

"Girl, you're not going to believe this. I work with her," Sherry informed me. "I can tell you where she works. I can tell you where she lives."

My cousin and I tried to figure out how to plot this all out. We had home phones, and back then we had a call return feature for calling folks back. For whatever reason, the young lady, who Mr. S was seeing, had called our house, and they were talking on the phone. I didn't know, but something told me when I saw him get off the phone that day to go back to the phone and get that number off the Caller ID. When I used the call return feature, the number came up. I saved it on my phone, then called back. Yes, I did, and I heard her voice.

After she picked up, I responded with, "Did you call for someone? This is the S residence." I was still trying to take it all in. *How can I handle this?* I went on to say, "Are you looking for me or my husband?" This is Mrs. S. She said, "I don't think so." I told her, "Well, I saw you were the last call, so I'm returning calls since my husband has me managing everything…Hahaha." I was making light of what I really felt. I then asked, "Who is this, by the way?" She said, "Shun B." I then thought to myself, *so Shun B is fellowshipping with my husband.* I'm now trying to figure out what to say next. Honestly, the conversation became fuzzy because once she said her name, I went into daydreaming about how I could possibly bring this relationship of theirs to an end.

By this time in their relationship, Mr. S had gotten extremely comfortable. He was taking our kids with him to spend the night at her place. I'm broken by all of this—yet trying to figure out my next move. Mr. S had also gotten comfortable about talking about this new relationship with another close friend of ours named Warren. The thing about it was, Mr. S was sharing aspects of their relationship with Warren, and Warren was sharing Mr. S's whereabouts with me.

What I didn't know was that Warren liked me romantically also and didn't have our marriage in our best interest when he offered to take me to the other woman's house to verify if my kids were there. The curiosity was driving me insane. Warren asked if I needed a ride since he saw I had made up my mind and was going to verify where my children were. He had heard most of what was happening because he was also always at our home and listening when I was conversing with my cousin, Sherry, about it. He was all-in for the suspense of it all. "You need to go over there. I can take you," he kept saying.

Warren and I got in the car and drove over there. There was my husband's car, and I knew he had our children with him. Mr. S never knew I was out there. I sat there thinking of all the things I could do, but it all amounted to GO HOME. You came and you saw. I was deeply hurt, somewhat accepting at this point that my husband no longer wanted to be my husband.

I needed to be able to do something, and I didn't know what it was. Sherry suggested going to her job to talk, so I remember calling the job, asking to speak to her. Someone told me she was with 'so and so,' which pretty much meant she was unavailable. I told the person on the other end of the phone, "Well, I really would like to speak with her. I have an appointment with her, so I'd like to know she's going to be there this time. I'll come by the office." They confirmed and rattled off all I needed to know. I went to the office. I had already found pics of her, so I knew exactly what she looked like, and there she was.

"Hi, my name is... Yeah, my last name is... and I'm here to find out what is going on with you and my husband. I don't know what he's told you, but we're happily married." *Yes, I exaggerated using the word happily.*

"Well, I don't know what he's told you, but we're not together like that, and you two need to get that straight. I don't want to be in the middle of this. You two need to work that out," she replied.

From what I understood of that conversation, she told me that whatever my husband and I had going on with each other, she was not the cause of it, and I needed to take care of that with him.

No she did not just play me like I played Chica. The very thing that I had done to Mr. S's girlfriend back in Minnesota was now happening to me as his wife.

Whoever sows to please their flesh, from the flesh will reap destruction; whoever sows to please the Spirit, from the Spirit will reap eternal life. (Galatians 6:8 NIV)

From here it started becoming more unbearable. This was when Mr. S had gotten so comfortable with the other relationship that he would blatantly pack the children up and take them to her house to spend the night. The children, of course didn't understand but would come back and tell me. My son was the oldest, so I'd ask him.

"G2, where were you?"

"We were at Daddy's friend's house," he would innocently reply.

G2 would naively tell it all, but he didn't know what he was saying. "We slept on the floor," he'd share with me. "We had toys, and they were watching TV." I still didn't have a plan on handling this. I would ask Mr. S about it, but he would ignore me to the point where it felt like he was wondering why I was even talking to him. He had checked out.

All this time, the only thing my parents kept telling me was, "Fight for your marriage." No one said to walk away from it; only, "It would be better for you if you weren't the one who left the marriage. If he's going to leave, let him leave, but you should not be the one," so that was my mindset. I was going to fight and hang in there. I didn't know what fighting looked like, but I was willing.

CHAPTER 13

Pride & Humiliation

As I alluded to in the beginning, one time my dad drove my stepmom and my siblings to my home at about 6:00 PM to spend the night. By midnight Mr. S still wasn't home. At 2:00 AM, he still wasn't home; the next morning, he still wasn't home. Again, I was embarrassed. That was the first time my parents ever saw his behavior firsthand, even though I was talking regularly about how he was probably working late. It was now out; everyone could see he was not coming home. The entire time I thought, *I'm so embarrassed.*

Aside from my thoughts, I didn't know how to feel. It was such a slap in the face because Mr. S had called me earlier from the dealership. I don't know if he asked me anything, but I do remember saying, "My family is coming to town to stay over." I guess he didn't want to be pressured or have to deal with my dad about us, so he decided, "I *ain't* coming home." Thinking about it now, I'm sure that's what he did. That was one of the most humiliating experiences I can remember. There were some great moments in my marriage I will never forget, but there are also some very hurtful ones that I will always remember—that was one of them.

The hours went by without him coming home. My dad is a night owl, so he was up all night, and I had to keep telling him Mr. S hadn't made it in. That was the first time he'd stayed out until the next evening. Normally, he would come home at about four or five in the morning, but this time, he didn't come home until the next day, and I couldn't believe my whole family witnessed it.

No one really said anything about it because no one really wanted to deal with it. My dad didn't know what to say. He could see how hurt I was, and he kept saying he was going to pray for me and us. After that day, Mr. S's staying out started to become more and more regular; every two or three days, he would be gone. Then, he would come home for a day or two. I felt that when the girlfriend traveled, he would come home, and when she was in town, he was with her because he would do it for about two or three days at a time. Now, mind you, I was dying inside, yet I kept going. I couldn't bring myself to show the despair my heart was feeling. I was dedicated to standing strong and quietly keeping things in. Then something else happened.

Around that time, I started feeling sick. I didn't know why, but I couldn't hold down food for even a second. I didn't feel sick enough to stay in bed; it was more like my stomach was increasingly upset to the point where I finally went to the doctor, and he told me, "You're pregnant." At that moment, I was like, *"What? Pregnant!"* I was surprised and somewhat happy because I wanted another baby, but I knew our relationship was shaky.

We had the abortion early in 1995, then a miscarriage in 1996. I had had G2 in 1997, and after two years, we had Elizabeth in 1999. That whole time, I wasn't on any birth control or anything else. Now, Elizabeth was two, and I was pregnant, and Mr. S was not coming home regularly. When I finally told him, he had surprised me unintentionally by coming home from work, and I asked him if we could go into the den to talk. He came in and sat down.

"I don't know if you're ready for this," I started, hoping he might be happy, "but we're pregnant."

His reaction was so negative that I remember thinking, *is this the man who said he wanted me to be the mother of his children.* I could not believe it. I don't know why I thought he was going to be excited. I thought the news that we were going to have another child would be the turnaround for him to hear. Nevertheless, he was shocked.

"What? Pregnant?" he asked.

"Yeah. We're pregnant," I replied.

Mr. S was like, "Oh, my God. What Titia?"

Oh, God? He showed deep disappointment. I looked at him, and he saw that I was distraught. *Did he just break me again?* I cringed. *He's not happy.* I so hoped this pregnancy was going to be the thing that would cause him to realize we had to figure us out, but no, that is not what he was thinking.

After the conversation ended, our regular habits began again. A couple of weeks later, we went to the doctor's office. Going with me to the doctor was something Mr. S decided he was doing. He wanted to know what was going on and to see if I was truly pregnant. He kept telling me, "I'm going to the doctor's appointments with you."

When I went to the doctor the first time, I was already four months pregnant. I started showing right away. Mr. S and I were still very unsteady, but he would come home when he wanted to be intimate with me and then be gone for another couple of days. I wasn't sure how to be. I just went along with the flow.

When we went back to the doctor together, they did a sonogram. The doctor searched around for a bit to see the baby. They could not find a heartbeat, so they asked us to come back in another two weeks. We went two weeks later, and they said the same thing, "We don't hear anything." They weren't saying anything negative; they just said, "This is weird. Maybe the baby is hiding behind something. Go home, give it two more weeks, and we'll see if the baby comes from hiding."

During that time of waiting, the doctor called. He then asked me to come in. This time I went alone. Once in his office he said, "Usually, around this term of pregnancy, numbers are at about 50,000, but yours are at about half a million, which says you have cancer." *Wait. What?*

"Cancer!" I exclaimed. "That doesn't make sense. That's crazy; that cannot be the case, seriously."

"The numbers don't lie," he told me. "You're at half a million, and you're not even halfway through your pregnancy. This reading is abnormal. The only way numbers move like that is if cancer is present."

The doctor kept saying to me, "Ma'am, it's officially cancer. These numbers don't happen unless it's cancer-related." *You're at half a million.* I was confused. It made no sense; however, he called it Choriocarcinoma, which is basically uterine cancer. I was told different things about the cancer process, then we started talking about treatment, but it all sounded very foreign to me. I just remember thinking *this cannot be happening.*

Later that day, I decided to go over to Tam and Kirk's house. "Y'all, the doctor said I have cancer," I told them.

They both looked at me like, *What? Are you serious?*

I repeated, "Yes. They're telling me I have uterine cancer."

Tam and Kirk asked me if I had informed Mr. S, but I told them, "No." They were the first people I spoke with about it.

"Do you think you need to tell him?" Kirk asked.

I knew Mr. S needed to know, but we were so distant. I wanted to be around people who would encourage me after hearing the diagnosis. Honestly, I wasn't sure if he would even care. Things were very uncertain between the two of us, and I think Tam and Kirk were trying to figure out how to help. I stayed at their house for hours, and then

Kirk said, "Jon and I are going to go talk to Mr. S. We're going to tell him that we need to talk to him. Y'all need some help." And so, they did. Kirk and Jon (Kirk's best friend) went and ministered to him for hours.

That was one of those moments you never forget because it changed everything; that was the game-changer for us. Kirk and Jon talked with Mr. S, and he was very humble with a sense of remorse over what had happened. When I called home to say I was on my way, he answered the phone.

"Hey, I was making sure you were there. I'm getting ready to come to the house," I told him.

"Titia, tell me what's wrong. Tell me what's going on with you. Tell me what they said," was all he said in response.

"I'll tell you when I get home."

"No, no. Tell me now. I want to know what's going on."

I strongly reiterated that I'd tell him when I got home. Mr. S became quiet and said nothing else. Something changed instantly. When I got home, I thought he would be awake for me to tell him what I found out, but he was asleep or at least acted as if he was. He stayed in the same position the whole night and never woke up—never said a thing, never had a conversation about it. He left the next day as usual.

I went back to Kirk, and I said, "When I got home, he didn't even want to talk." Kirk told me to tell him exactly what had happened, and I did.

"I called Mr. S and said I was coming home, and he asked me what had happened. I told him I would tell him when I got home."

Then, Kirk said, "See, you did it again, Titia. You've got to understand; the man was in a position to hear you, and you put him off again. You're saying, 'wait, I don't want to talk about it on your time; I want to talk about it on my time.' That's what he's sick of. You don't even realize you're ruining everything."

From Mr. S's perspective, he was ready to talk to me on the phone, but I was making him wait and being in control again. This whole experience was eye-opening for me. They already knew he was wrong, but what they were saying beyond that was, "Titia, you played a major role in why he does what he does because you're so strong," and I didn't realize it.

There were many other instances where I was in control when decisions were being made in our home. It was all the little things I was saying we weren't doing... "We're not going here," or "I don't want to go to that party," or even "I don't want to be with your friends." I wasn't trying to have a conversation about anything. I was too busy directing where we were going. For Kirk, even though he knew about how negative my response was, he needed me to see it for myself. Kirk said to me, "This was not just about you; he was ready. Regardless of what you all were going through, he was ready, and you basically said, 'not now.' That was your window."

When I didn't tell Mr. S about my diagnosis on the phone, he had nothing else to do with me regarding that situation. He felt I could handle it. We did go back to the doctor one more time. For whatever reason, he still felt the need to go with me. I think he was still trying to see what was going on because once Kirk and Jon told him I had cancer, Mr. S was in disbelief and now wanted to hear it from me.

"I need to hear it from you," he said simply. "I know what they said, but I need to know what the doctor said to you. What did he tell you? What's going on?"

I responded, "We're pregnant, and I have uterine cancer."

After that, I remember Mr. S saying my family would be there for me, and I would have support from them. I quietly wept to myself thinking about how detached he was from caring about me at this point as we headed to our home for him to drop me off.

When I didn't improve, we went back to the doctor. My numbers were still outrageous and increasing rapidly. When they did another sonogram, there was still no heartbeat from the baby; something was very wrong. The doctors kept saying, "Something isn't right." It was abnormal because my body was growing, so for me to look pregnant and them not to hear a heartbeat was confusing. My body was preparing for a baby, but each time I went to the doctor, they kept saying they couldn't see one, and they couldn't hear one; they didn't know what was going on.

They ran more tests and still found nothing. By this time, my dad and my stepmother had started looking into holistic methods of dealing with cancer because they are what I call *"Natural Health Google."* Anything you want to know about health, herbs, and things of that nature, they are the Google for it. That's their area of expertise and their mentality for natural healing.

Eventually, my dad and stepmother asked me to start Ozone Therapy. This was a natural therapy for cancer treatment. Once I became more educated about it and realized I didn't want any of the doctor's recommendations, I started going three or four times a week. The distance was about an hour and a half away from me. The facility was Hale & Hearty (Pat Austin) in North Richland Hills, Texas, and at the time, they provided treatment in her home. It took a while to get there, but for me, I was fine. I had nothing to do, and I was thinking, *Cancer. Lord, I am trusting You. I'm not doing any of the treatments the doctors are telling me I need to be doing, so You've got to come up with something.* This was it. Ozone Therapy was the "something" the Lord came up with and had given me to do through my parents.

I started natural treatment, and people began praying for and with me. Another occurrence I'll never forget was when I walked into my church for Bible study one Wednesday evening, and they were calling my name at the same time. "Is Titia in the building? Is Titia here?" I happened to be walking in, and I questioned no one in particular, "Are they saying my name?" I literally walked down to the front, and Dr. Tony Evans had the whole church pray over me that night. I thought, *oh, my God.* That's when it hit me; this was serious. People had to pray for me because this was severe. Reality set in that I needed to take it even more seriously.

During this season, I was really getting closer to the Lord because I was doing so much praying about Mr. S that it wasn't even funny. DeAnna, my mentor, was sharing the Word with me regularly and holding me accountable. I was in the Bible all the time, trying to understand what the Lord was saying and where the answers were to the things I was dealing with—even though I was still struggling. I tried to figure out where in the *Word* would it tell me to do something, and I heard the Lord tell me He was getting ready to heal my body.

I started telling everyone what He said. "The Lord is going to heal me. He spoke it to me. I'm clear about it," I told Mr. S. He was like, "Psshh, whatever," and acted like he didn't even care. Mr. S didn't believe I would be healed because the last time we'd gone to the doctor, right after I started getting sicker, the doctor had said, "Your cancer has aborted your pregnancy. That's why we can't see the growth. Your body doesn't know you're not pregnant anymore, so it's still growing."

It was considered a mole pregnancy. I could have just gone ahead and lost my mind at that point. My husband was in another full-fledged relationship, and my body had aborted our baby due to cancer. It was all too much.

I tried to put all of that out of my head because I didn't want to deal with it anymore. I *really* tried to put it all somewhere way back in my mind. The medical team told me I was going to need surgery because they needed to remove the growths due to all that was going on inside of me. There hadn't been a passing of anything at all, and I was still carrying my lifeless, unborn baby around, not even knowing so much was taking place in my body. I just knew I was sick, unable to keep anything down. My body was still growing. It was unbelievable, and I was a rare case. I looked every bit of 6 months pregnant, and the growth did not stop.

CHAPTER 14

An Issue of Blood

There was another problem that started to occur—bleeding. I started hemorrhaging uncontrollably every single day. Because my cycles had been irregular over the years, nothing usually surprised me, but this was non-stop bleeding. I would bleed at any time of day or night. It was overwhelming and disconcerting at the same time. I spent quite a bit of time at home since I never knew when the bleeding would begin or end. This went on for six weeks straight until I could get enough iron injections to be well enough to have surgery. I had become somewhat tired and weary, yet I just kept praying and asking the Lord to keep me.

It was now time for me to have surgery. I asked them to take out whatever they could at that point to stop the bleeding. The surgery was successful. *Thank you, Jesus!* The bleeding finally stopped. Afterward, I was still going through Ozone Therapy and started going back to the doctor to check the numbers for the cancer. I went for three more months, and each time I went, they said, "Your numbers are decreasing! Your numbers are decreasing!"

I'd gone from half a million to 100,000 or less, and then to maybe 50,000 less, and it was rapidly decreasing. The medical experts were amazed and asked, "What has happened? What did you do?" They'd tried to get me to do radiation and other treatments, but I chose to continue going to Ozone Therapy. I always went back to the doctor just for them to see what my numbers were, but that was the only reason I needed to go. We wanted to verify what was going on with me and to see if the Ozone was helpful.

The last time I went to the doctor, I called my mom and her friend, EarLane, who happened to be together that day. I told them, "Well, I'm going to the doctor, and they're gonna tell me where I'm at with my numbers. You should meet us there." Mr. S took me, and they met us. While he and I waited in the car, I was emotionally pleading with him.

"Why can't we work this out? We have a family."

He ultimately said, "Your family will be there for you." He just meant without him.

It was apparent I was wasting my time because he had emotionally moved on. I wrapped my mind around that. *He has moved on.* After we got settled and went inside with my mom and her friend, the doctor told us, "You are now between ten and zero, so you are officially cancer-free." Immediately, I went into worship at the hospital. *I feel it like it was yesterday.* I lost it in there. I lost it, and my mom couldn't believe it.

She and EarLane started rejoicing with me. When I looked over at Mr. S, all he had to say was, "When are we leaving?" *Wow.* I was baffled on how to respond to him anymore. I didn't know what to be to him now, so I started becoming his puppet. I'd move on in my mind for five minutes then I'd be right back trying again. "Okay, do I need to fix my hair differently? Do I need to wear a certain outfit?" I would ask myself. I was trying to think of anything I could do to hold my marriage together. I was fighting and holding on because I was looking at my children and telling myself, "This has to be a phase; this has to be temporary. It cannot be permanent."

That went on for weeks, and then it started to hit me. I realized I could not live like that and wondered how I'd become so miserable that I'd lost myself completely, to the point where I couldn't comprehend how to respond to him anymore. *I want y'all to understand I thought I was trying to keep it all together.* I felt like a zombie. Was I awake or asleep, alive, or dead? That was my thought process, always wondering because I was lost. I talked to my family and friends to get help, but they couldn't really help at that time.

Mr. S stopped listening to anyone, and he didn't want to talk to anyone either. Different people tried to talk to him, or at least *wanted* to talk to him, but he never budged. My pastor, Dr. Tony Evans, had even called him several times for a meeting, and he stood him up. He would constantly tell Dr. Evans he was coming, but he kept rescheduling. I would warn Dr. Evans that Mr. S may not come, but he would say, "That's okay, I'm not going to give up on you guys."

It finally got to the point where Dr. Evans told me, "I can't make him come." It had been three or four times that I had scheduled a meeting, and Mr. S said he would come but didn't. That's when I started feeling like we really were ending. I wasn't sure what was about to happen, but the many nights Mr. S didn't come home, I continued to pray. I'd be praying in my closet, crying to the Lord, saying, "Father, I'm clueless as to what I should be doing. Help me. Help us. I'm losing my husband." Afterward, I clearly heard the Lord say, "Ask him for forgiveness," one night when Mr. S had taken the kids to stay at his girlfriend's house.

"Titia, ask him for forgiveness."

"Not today, Lord," I responded. "That's *not* happening. He does not deserve it. I am not saying I'm sorry to him again—by no means, whatsoever." *As much as I thought I wanted my marriage, the thought of asking Mr. S to forgive me was incomprehensible. I asked the Lord for help but didn't want to obey His command. Still wanting answers on my terms. (Oh, foolish woman.)*

I stood firm on that, and I meant it. At the time, I did not have any fear of what I was saying. (After all of this I was still just as ignorant.) In my mind, I thought me saying no to the Lord was just like me saying no to anyone else. *Wrong again!* It was so much bigger than that.

Playing with My Emotions

By now, we were putting our house back on the market. We had a For Sale sign in the yard, and the realtor was coming to meet with us. Mr. S had to come home that morning to meet us. We were sitting at the table in our formal dining area, and the realtor came and sat with us. We were going over the paperwork, and he was busy telling us what we needed to do to get the house together to sell it. We went through that meeting, and I don't know what the transition was, but Mr. S realized that maybe we were making a mistake.

I could not predict what would happen next. After the realtor left, Mr. S told me, "The devil almost had me, and I don't want to lose my family. I love you, and I don't know what got into me." I sat there trying to figure out what had just happened and trying to take all this in, but he kept talking. "I'm going to get my stuff, and I'm going to come back home." I was sitting there in disbelief and gratitude at the same time. Just like that, Mr. S had realized he wanted his family.

"Well, please take G2 with you," I said. "I don't want you going by yourself to get your things."

Mr. S agreed. Then he went and got his things. I asked him to take G2 because I felt that was my assurance they would come back home. When they returned, I saw our truck filled up with all his stuff. I was amazed and distressed when I saw all the items he had been quietly removing from our home and taking to hers. I would never have known if I had not seen it for myself. I was too busy trying to not focus on him that I *didn't see any* of that—not one piece of it did I ever see leave. There were so many items. It was all different things he had secretly removed. Seeing that was proof that Mr. S was creating a new life with someone else. That was not just a phase, as I so foolishly believed.

At any rate, we dealt with the return of his things briefly. I deeply wanted us to see someone and to get some help. I said to Mr. S, "I really would like for us to get some counseling."

Well I noticed his attitude was a little different. At first, before he and G2 left for her house, he was remorseful and apologetic, but when they came back, he was very dismissive. I was confused, yet I didn't want to rock the boat, so I just went along with what he dictated at that point.

We got the kids together, put them into the car, and went to get food at the grocery store, which was something he liked to do. I was thinking, *okay, this is family night. We're at the grocery store. This is good.* When we got back to the house—and this was the flipper—it was time for us to get ready to go to bed. He said, "I'm going to sleep upstairs with G2." I was thoroughly perplexed but agreed. Again I wanted everything smooth that night, so I told him, "Okay." The next day Mr. S went to work.

"I'll see you this evening around 5:00 PM," he informed me before he left.

"Okay, that sounds good," I replied.

DeAnna recommended that I send him flowers at work because I wanted him to know how grateful I was that he was back with his family. I sent the flowers, and I called the flower place later to confirm delivery. They answered in the affirmative. I spent the rest of the time wondering if and hoping that he would soon call me.

Five o'clock had come and gone, and I didn't hear from him. Six o'clock came and went; still, I didn't hear from him. When I called him, Mr. S didn't answer the phone. I told myself, "Okay, this is weird." Another hour went by, and I called him again. He still didn't answer. Now my chest was starting to tighten from concern. By this time, it was 8:45 PM, and he finally answered the phone.

"Hey, what's going on? Did you get the flowers?" I asked.

He replied, "I can't do this."

"What?"

"I can't do this," he repeated. "It's not going to work; this marriage is not going to work. No, it's not going to work."

My heart dropped and I broke down because I had been hopefully waiting for him with the anticipation of us being a family again, and he said he couldn't do it. I felt crumbled. His whole attitude had changed, and I could hear his dedication to moving on. I lowered my head and simply said, "Okay." We hung up the phone, and that was it. Then, I completely lost it. I cried, and I cried. The next day when he came home, I was still crying.

I asked him, point-blank, "Why are you doing this? I don't understand what's happening."

CHAPTER 15

Emasculation Cuts

S itting on the edge of the bed, Mr. S opened up. "You have emasculated me. I feel less than a man when it comes to you. I feel like you run everything. It's been about you, and you can't see it."

I sat in front of him, kneeling as I cried and pleaded. "I didn't realize. I had no idea." We sat there a while as I cried, and he quietly watched me with such sadness. He ended up leaving anyway, and I realized that was it.

Within 24 hours, Mr. S had removed all the money out of my checking account. I was devastated when I tried to get gas, and my card didn't work. I thought *that's weird.* I tried another one; that one wasn't working either. I wasn't working at the time, so I told myself, "This is not happening. I know this is not happening." This all felt unreal. It felt like a movie because you never dream that the things you see on TV are now happening to you.

I called my parents, and I told my mom I was going to need some help. Her immediate response was, "You need to go and get a temporary child support order because he cannot just take all your money. You need to go ahead and start procedures right away." I thought about how fast all of this was happening—too fast. *And now my mom and I are talking about me getting temporary orders.*

I called an attorney, and she told me I needed $5,000 as a retainer fee. *$5000?!?!* Where was I getting that kind of money? I had some money saved and ended up borrowing the rest.

The attorney told me she could get me the help I needed. She ended up doing that and was also able to get the temporary order, which generally doesn't happen until there is a divorce filed. Three days later, there was a knock on my door; it was the bailiff bringing divorce papers. I was thinking, *this is too much.* What is happening? What am I supposed to do next? Once again, my mind was all over the place. It was one thing after another. When I received those divorce papers, I was even more devastated, yet I accepted it and put on my big girl pants and started my *moving on* plan. Shortly after that, I asked Mr. S what his schedule was.

"I'm going to be working late tonight," he told me.

"Okay, what about tomorrow?" I asked.

"I don't even know if I'll be home."

That usually meant he was staying with his girlfriend. I told him, okay, because I'd only asked for his schedule so that I could move out. If he wasn't going to be there, we wouldn't be doing any quarreling. I didn't want to be stuck with the house and its payment being that I didn't have consistent additional income, and I'd found a Townhome not far from our house already. It was maybe six minutes away to be close to the children's school, and I'd already put a deposit down on it. The plan was to get moved out by the time Mr. S would return from his girlfriend's. He ended up coming in late that night, so the next morning when he left for work, about 20 of my friends came over to help me move within minutes of him leaving. By the time I thought he would have been off work, we had already moved out.

I called Mr. S that night to tell him the kids and I had moved. I could hear in his voice that he didn't believe me, although he essentially let me know it wasn't a big deal. However, two days later, when he finally came home and walked into the half-empty house with no family and saw that we had left for good, he was livid and called me.

"Bring all my stuff back!" he yelled at the top of his lungs.

"I moved out on Monday, and you're just now seeing this?" I inquired.

He went off on me, but I didn't care at that point. It was apparent he hadn't been home. All I could think was *you've been with another woman, and you have the nerve to be upset.* He could say what he wanted to. I had peace of mind about moving out, and that's how sleep began again for me.

I hadn't realized that for seven years, I hadn't slept peacefully; I'd only experienced naps. I would take long naps, here and there, because I could not rest regularly. When I moved into the Townhome, the first night I went to sleep and slept all night. *Something must be wrong with me*, I thought. *I need to make sure I'm not sick. I've got to go to the doctor.*

The next night, I went to bed again, and I slept all night *again*. It happened two times in a row. I called my mom.

"I slept. I think something's wrong with me," I said, genuinely worried.

"Girl, you're supposed to sleep," she laughed.

"No, no," I told her. "No, you're not. I don't *ever* sleep. I stay awake all night."

Mom thought I was crazy because I shared with her for about two weeks. I couldn't believe I was going to sleep every night and resting because I had gotten so used to dealing with worry, in addition to all the other stuff that kept me up.

I soon saw that even though I wasn't the breadwinner, I was the bill payer. I had managed all the bills. Mr. S literally said, "Here's the money. Handle it." That was plenty of pressure on me because we had a lot of bills. He felt he could sleep because I would handle it. He wanted me to manage it all but at the same time, he wasn't feeling it when I did. I don't think he knew what he wanted. I honestly don't think either of us knew what we were *both* doing and responsible for. It was all out of order, as was the foundation. Everything about it was wrong. You put two blind and foolish people together, and you're going to get a whole bunch of foolery, which kept me awake for seven years. When I got settled in at the new place, I didn't even tell him where we lived right away. I waited until it was time for him to bring the kids home the following week.

When Mr. S brought the kids back to our new home, he had become furious and bitter. I had also taken some funds from an insurance claim to assist me in times like these I didn't tell him about, but the insurance company made him aware. Nothing about me was right nor good in his sight, at that point.

From then on, he'd always have something to say about how I was raising the kids. For instance, "What's wrong with their clothes? Why is Elizabeth's hair looking like this? You don't have them in bed by six." To him, I was such a horrible mom. There was nothing I could do right. The complaints went on for about the next six years; every time he would call, it would get on my last nerve. Elizabeth could be taking a bath. "Why are you not in there watching her?" he complained.

It didn't matter what was happening; Mr. S was going to find something wrong. He made sure he told everyone I was a horrible mom. I just learned to ignore him. When people asked him about the divorce and why he was doing it, he said, "I don't even know if our son, G2, is mine."

That's what he told his family and mine. I couldn't believe that's what he was saying. I also couldn't believe he really thought that was true and didn't know why he would wonder for the last five years instead of saying something. My response was, "Go find out if you don't know if he's your son. There are ways to find out."

At the end of it all, he just wanted to make sure I looked like the bad person who had caused the divorce, and it worked for his family. He convinced people he believed he was making the right decision. After a year had gone by, we finalized our divorce in February of 2002, and I was no longer Mr. S's wife. Within two years of the final decree, he moved back to his hometown, and I was officially a single parent.

Fast forward to 2018. By this time, I had founded a homeless organization (Where Are You Outreach) and had been serving for several years. I received an email telling me I had been nominated to receive a grant for the organization. I was also working at KHVN radio station here in Dallas, and James Thomas from *Southern Dallas Magazine* was there when I told him about the grant nomination. He asked if I knew someone whose name sounded familiar, but I didn't know for sure. "Well, she's a big wig at a well-known bank," he said.

I asked James if she was from Dallas, and he said, "Yes. Her family has an organization where they give back to the students who need scholarships and things like that." I thought that was cool and decided to complete the forms for the grant to see if we would get approved. Something told me to go and look at the organization, so I went and researched it.

I saw the name of the founder, and I questioned why I knew it. I kept looking at the picture, and I kept looking at the name because the first name was the same, but the last name was different. That first name stood out; it could only be one person. *This is amazing that this is happening right now,* I thought. I went to the philanthropist event, saw the person, and I said to myself, "Oh, my God. This is the woman my now children's father, Mr. S, was cheating with. Is she about to give me an award? That is absolutely amazing."

I told my current husband, John Wayne Owens (who I will tell y'all about at the end), "Honey, let me tell you what's about to happen because I don't want you to be surprised. I don't know if she remembers me. I'm not sure, but if she does, I want you prepared."

"Wow, that's crazy," is all he kept saying. "She's about to give you some money *and* an award."

I had to go to God and say, "Okay, Lord, what is this? Why are You allowing this?" He used JWayne to tell me, "You need to make sure you have every bit of forgiveness in your heart. You should have no unforgiveness within you. Keep your slate clean. He's making sure that even in this situation, you have nothing inside of you that looks like unforgiveness."

When I'd walked in earlier and saw her, I couldn't believe it. I didn't know if she knew or remembered me. We didn't address anything, so I don't particularly know if she realized it was me or not. When she gave me the award, she just kept saying, "Thank you so much," and I said the same thing to her. I was genuinely grateful that we were being blessed to assist the homeless regardless of how it came. I believe this night was most assuredly a test, and I just pray I pleased the Lord with my response.

When God started playing back the movie of my life, my children's father played a role in this, yet I had so much more to do with it. God was showing me things that went far beyond him and had so much to do with:

- **How I** started the foundation,

- **How I** played games,

- **How I** responded to him,

- **How I** dismissed him on many levels,

- **How I** ignored anything he said,

- **How I** used status to compete, and

- **How I** disobeyed God.

I couldn't see my strong will because I was so into me at the time. That's where I was, and I believe now—as horrible as it was—that my ex-husband was the tool God used to break me because I had elevated myself. I was elevated, in my mind, and it went to my head. It had happened for different reasons, like the fact that I was talented and trained to a do a variety of things (i.e., hair, make-up, sing, studio work, etc.) and had gone to a performing arts school (Arts Magnet) where they fed our egos and boosted our self-confidence. Then I moved to Minnesota, where we were treated as superstars because we were the only African American female group on the scene at the time. All of these factors perpetuated my arrogance.

My world changed. That's what happened when God broke me to a place where I was just thankful, but there was a time when I would just know, *yeah, I'm going to win. I'm about to get this.* It wasn't because of my faith in God; I was just arrogant. I didn't realize how bad I was, and breaking those characteristics wasn't going to happen on my own.

Knowing now what I know about myself, a scripture comes to mind that talks about an undisciplined child—how rotten they are or how out of control they can be. That's what I was. I was an undisciplined child. I could talk my way out of getting into trouble. I was the Queen of Sneak. (Get ready for that book.) That's why I am such a disciplinarian. All my friends know if they're having issues with their children to bring them to me, and I will deal with them because I know what you can get into if you don't get the necessary discipline. After all, I was dying from undiscipline. I really was.

I didn't know how bad I was, and that's why I stayed on my children. I didn't want them to have the same undisciplined struggles I had. I would say, "Don't bring your children over to my house and think they are not going to get disciplined if necessary." *I don't spare the rod.* Usually, I don't have to use one because they know when I'm serious and when I'm playing. They know it's better not to gamble with me, so they don't do whatever 'it is' they're considering.

When my children were younger, that was my reputation because I'd even discipline children I didn't know. They could be at school, and I'd be telling them, "Come here; why are your pants down?" I'd get an "oh, I'm sorry" because I would say it stern enough and serious enough. It's because I understand the severity of a lack of discipline. I've also learned there has to be a balance when disciplining. There should be just as much encouragement and applause for the good done also.

I learned my lessons the hard way, so now, when I see an undisciplined child or a parent being passive with their children, it does something to me. In my mind, I'm going *you don't know what you're doing. You are setting that child up to fail, and you don't even know it.*

I was not clear on this whole marriage thing. I had no clue, and even though I lived with my parents, I didn't see them personally interact until my marriage was over. I didn't see them as models; I can't say I was looking either.

I saw my mom work, and my stepfather ran the church. I could see they worked well together and they both managed things. In terms of my dad and my stepmother, my dad was always in the room with us talking, so I saw him interact with his wife while we were all sitting around watching TV or talking. I just knew my dad was hilarious and enjoyed connecting with others. He openly shared about his past and the many foolish things he had done over his lifetime. He shared regularly, but he still wasn't communicating what a wife is supposed to be.

I literally was clueless—clueless and ignorant, with no idea whatsoever about being a wife, and I *very much* learned the hard way. I had to go through all this foolishness to become broken and unlearn my foolish ways. My selfishness and my lack of humility caused me to get rid of a man.

CHAPTER 16

Tools to Prepare for Marriage

I would like to answer someone who may be asking, "How can I prepare for my marriage?" Well, you can prepare by not necessarily trying to imitate anyone else because your marriage will be *your* marriage. Equip yourself by reading the Word, getting godly counsel, reading about marriage, and learning from older couples with wisdom because you do *need to know* how to deal with certain issues that will inevitably arise. You need to know the guidelines and that who you are in Christ is the foundation and the key. Look up the biblical definition of grace and learn that grace will be a regular rescue. You can never really know what's coming next, but you can know the Word to assist you when challenges come. Our foundation was so wrong that we had little advantage.

My dear friend Victoria always says you need to identify the majors and minors upfront, even though you will never know everything about your mate. Nevertheless, the benefit of confronting some of the dealbreakers upfront is dealing with it then, as opposed to knowing they're dealbreakers and going along with them. For example, I saw commitment issues and concerns upfront, and I still ignored it to some degree. You must pay attention and see that everything negative can eventually get worse. Just know that up front.

Every wife will probably tell you that anything the husband is doing negatively upfront will probably not get any better. They usually get worse unless the Lord knocks them over the head with the Holy Spirit and tells them how miraculous you are. Even so, that sometimes takes a long time. The good thing is that whatever they're good at, they usually remain good at. Fortunately, some things stay the same.

When I was in the pre-stages of marriage, I should have been setting the tone, but I was in a fake mode of performing so that he could think I cooked and cleaned instead of just being myself. For you, the essential things will be:

- Know who you are in Christ;
- Be honest;
- Look at things clearly;
- See him for who he truly is;
- Be able to talk about concerns;
- Seek to know his heart;
- Listen *plenty; and*
- Do NOT overlook dealbreakers.

There is going to have to be a lot of communication taking place. I would say to have godly counsel in the process of building a connection.

If someone is seriously in your life for a predestined relationship, then you *definitely* want to have someone around you who can speak the Word into it, observe it, and be open to listening. Remember, I was waiting for someone to tell me what they actually saw or whatever the truth was, but many assumed I wouldn't listen, and maybe I wouldn't have. Unfortunately, I only listened mostly when I felt desperate.

Regardless, you want godly counsel. You want to start talking to people who have been or are already married because they will tell you different things from their experiences. They'll drop nuggets; everyone's will be different. Even reading on marriage will be different. There's an excellent book called *Choosing God's Best*, which I very much recommend you read. I read it before I met my current husband. In fact, we read it together when we were dating.

Always remember the Lord cares about us. Yes, He hears your cry. It took me a long time to receive others coaching me with these words because my heart was so hardened, and I was not taking others at their word when they would say stuff like, "Spend more time praying for him. Spend more time on your knees. Spend more time in the Lord." I heard that, but I felt like *that's not going to work. I need to help Mr. S out a little bit.* That's what I would say, but when I started to try it and really believed it and started praying, I did see the change.

Many times, if we are used to being in control, it can take longer to let it go. That's the battle we have; we know how to make things happen. Yet it doesn't always work, not with men. Men don't always move when we want them to, and if they do, sometimes they're doing it out of anger or frustration, and you don't want that. That's why I'm telling you it's a big deal to be praying for your man. I even want you to practice praying for him even before he, your husband, comes. Please pray for yourself and constantly examine yourself with God's standards.

Right now, I pray for my children's future husband and wife all the time. I started asking the Lord when they were kids to provide them with a godly husband and a godly wife because I know how important it is to have a mate who desires to please the Lord. That means they would be willing to work it out with an understanding that at the center—the Lord is the answer. That's something I didn't have in my first marriage.

I'm going to say the redemption for me has been my children. Looking at how Mr. S communicated that I was such a horrible mother once we were divorced, to see the outcome of my children has been nothing but a blessing to me. They don't even know the half of it. (Well until now.)

All I can say is, "Thank You, Lord." I'm always telling my son and my daughter how I get emotional talking about them. When I see who they are as Believers—how they love and how they serve—I can't help but be proud. Especially knowing how Mr. S negatively communicated about my mothering and my parenting—*even though he decided I was going to be the mother of his children.* To see our children now, to see how God has blessed them, it is utterly amazing. I'm very blessed and grateful.

Mr. S now says he's proud of them and that I've done a great job with the kids since they have both graduated and have productive lives. I was grateful for those words, but it took me a long time not to need them.

It took me a long time to be okay with whether he said it or not; at first, I wanted him to acknowledge or recognize it, but my children ended up doing it for me. Being who they are and seeing all the spiritual growth they have received—and the blessing and favor that God has had on their lives—it's just been rewarding. I believe God is still giving me grace because it was undeserved, looking at my past.

I shared how God wanted me to apologize to Mr. S once, and I refused. I refused due to feeling he didn't deserve it. Again, that was a decision I convinced myself was right. I had criticized, rationalized, and only looked at what he had done. Yet, when Mr. S told me I had emasculated him, I didn't hesitate to say I was sorry. I was clueless, and I felt awful. Oh, and let me tell you; there were consequences to the action of telling God no if you haven't received that word yet. The discipline went on for years!

As a little girl I personally watched Cinderella so many times that one of my dreams was to be a wife, but I had no idea what a wife was—not a clue. As we know, you can have all the highest intentions, but how foolish I was. There were so many lessons I needed to learn. Please don't misunderstand, I wasn't a constant monster, and I really wanted to be married to Mr. S. As you have read, a huge problem was the foundation laid that created much bigger problems than we knew how to handle.

Looking back at the younger me now, I see who I was then, and I believe it could have been different. Back then, it was going to go the way I preferred it—period. Of course, he had the choice not to follow the direction I pulled him in. I was just dictating what our life was going to be concerning the decisions I made. I navigated the road I wanted to take to get to where I wanted to be—good or bad.

Along the way, however, after a few years of marriage, I put a halt to the games. I gave up and did not want to play any more games. I had become worn out from trying different methods to fix us as well as trying to keep the façade that we were fine. I can't say we were ever working on our relationship at the same time, so I surrendered, and I ended up losing because Christ was not leading; I was. When I did wave the white flag to surrender, Mr. S didn't like that person because even he was at least enjoying the challenge.

At the foundation of the relationship, I painted a façade before we ever got married, like a lot of women do. In other words, we pretend we can cook; we pretend we are clean; we pretend we're able to follow. We also pretend that we're kind, and we pretend that we do what the men in our lives ask. We play make-believe, then when we get married, we decide we don't have to do all that anymore. Now I realize all women don't do this, but a lot of them do.

When we have stopped pretending, they're still the same person, still believing our façade, and they're trying to figure out who we've become now that we're saying, "I don't clean up, and I don't cook. I was just doing that to impress you." In some way, we get this vision of them needing to see us as this great potential wife when, in actuality, they need to see the real you.

That's one of the major reasons we bumped heads so much. He was trying to figure out who he married because I continued to play games with him. I was again doing what my dad had taught me. That wasn't how to be a wife. He had taught me how to win—with games being the foundation.

Many couples go to counseling when problems arise, but we did not. I also saw other things I chose to ignore early on that didn't get addressed. Like, he wasn't blatantly cheating while we were dating, but even before we were married, the ex-girlfriend's excessive calling and connections to his past girlfriends needed to end.

I should have communicated clearly that I didn't like it when we were dating. I've learned that you have to express yourself and say those things upfront. If they don't like it, then you have to decide whether you can live with it. If you express your dislikes and your partner continues to do it, you must then determine if it is something you can live with. Whatever you allow in your relationship will continue.

Be honest with yourself. There is no place for deception. I didn't know who I was, so part of me didn't know what would've happened if he had told me I was a game-player. That's what I was good at—playing a game. I wasn't good at knowing him, listening to him, hearing his heart, or believing in what he said. That wasn't who I was. What I could do was smile and internally yell, "Checkmate. I just won." That was my strength, which is not the way you enter into a relationship.

Many people are very immature when they're starting the "seriously dating" process unless they have godly people around them or have already trained themselves in some form of Christ-centered wisdom. For example, I was in the homes of people who were in church, but I never heard relationship conversations or saw a relationship I valued in action. I didn't discuss relationships. They were around, but they weren't big on communicating.

I repeat. Even when you're not intentionally training a person, you're still training a person. What we watch others do and retain for ourselves, that info is usually what we imitate. Most people are not taught commitment; they simply learn to get out there and move around.

The prevailing mindset for young people is not to commit until they are older. I think boys are taught this more often than girls. I don't believe Mr. S thought he was hurting me; he was doing what he apparently was used to. Our relationship wasn't too farfetched, but our beliefs were. Unrealistic expectations, amongst other things, also contributed a great deal to our divorce. There was no commitment to protecting our marriage, protecting our relationship, or a commitment to growth and change. I was married to a professional athlete, so he came with his own expectations altogether, and I went and created some we didn't actually sit down and talk about for ourselves.

I do not blame Mr. S. We both made mistakes. We both made bad choices which caused great consequences. Our greatest reward was our children, and I am eternally grateful for that. My children taught me to be more selfless and compassionate through their kindness and unconditional love. The Lord restored marriage through my current husband, John Wayne Owens, and I cannot thank Him enough for giving me the opportunity to retake the wife exam for a lifetime.

I had allowed everything to happen up until the very end and still didn't know how I was supposed to respond when it did. I hadn't planned on playing so many games. When it started, I figured we would go through this phase until we got tired of doing it. I thought that was what I was supposed to do until after it was all over when people came to me and started with, "Well, you should have…"

I still need a lot of work. However, the Lord keeps stripping off the sin nature daily and I give the Lord permission to use me however He chooses. My past, while at times unpleasant, has helped mold me into the marriage coach I am today. It was those experiences that have equipped me to help build and sustain successful marriages. I am a vessel put on this earth to be used by Him and for Him. To God be the glory for allowing me to share this journey. It was HARD, yet it was WORTH IT.

TO GOD BE THE GLORY!!! WE DID IT!!!

Lulanger's Memory

I'd like to share a bit more about my brother, Lulanger Webb Washington, III. Lulanger passed on back in 2008. He'd had diabetes since he was 11 years old and died at the age of 35. He had lost his sight three years before he passed and was on dialysis, and when he did pass, he had gone into a diabetic coma.

Lulanger was found under his bed when he died. The very night before that happened, he had called and told me something similar in the frail voice I still remember. "Titia, I went to sleep; my sugar must have been out of control. When I woke up, I was under the bed," he said. "I don't know how I got there." That was the night before he died. The next night it happened again, except he didn't wake up.

Before that, my brother had always been more like a son to me. He was never really a brother. When he was incredibly young, I wasn't too fond of him because my mom always made me keep him whenever she was at work. My first stepfather, JW, was at work, too, and since I was the oldest, my brother was my responsibility.

When we started visiting my dad during the summers, Dad would say to me, "You need to love your brother. You need to love your sisters. You need to love your mom." He said that often. I heard it all my life, but it took me a while to start listening to it and saying to myself, "I need to love my brother and take care of him." Over the years, some type of transition happened to where I started realizing I did need to love and take care of him. I don't know when the transition occurred; I just embraced it, and we ended up being remarkably close.

I remember realizing Lulanger was sick when we were at home one Christmas opening gifts, and he began to lose consciousness. I was going, "Hey, hey! Wake up!" He would then say, "Okay, okay." It happened two or three times, so I said, "Mom, he's not opening up his gifts." I had never known about sickness before. At that time, he was 11, and I was 14, so I didn't understand what sickness even looked like. No one in my family had ever been sick for me to know what that was; I just knew something was wrong with him.

My mom came inside and saw my brother, and we rushed him to the hospital. He was diagnosed with diabetes and had to inject three shots of insulin a day for the rest of his life. Since the doctor suggested that Lulanger needed to be independent, we all followed that direction. Even though he was now sick, my mom concluded, "this isn't easy to handle." The doctors recommended that Lulanger learn how to take care of himself, and that was that.

Lulanger took care of his diabetes all his life. All the test-taking and blood sugar checks, he did them himself. I was never taught how to give him shots or check his sugar until months before he passed. I didn't help him with the shots, but I did assist him in his life with making sure he ate and financially assisting him.

"Make sure you get your supply." I was that person. I was also the "you need to get some sleep right now" or the "okay, you need to get up" person. I was the visual monitor who watched him and told him things like, "Your eyes are looking a little different. You need to eat." I could look at him and know he needed to eat right away. That was my role in his life, and he had become very dependent on me, even though he was still taking care of himself. I was the sister-mom who checked on him regularly, cared for him deeply, and loved him "tremenzingly."

My brother was one of the most talented individuals—this side of heaven. He was always the life of the party whether you wanted it or not. He was a singer, a cook, fashion designer, a mascot, dancer, comedian, and adored by me. We were each other's cheerleader, and we always had each other's back. If he were here, I'm sure he would say, "Make sure there's a section about me in your book." I can also hear him telling me how proud he is of me for being so transparent.

This part of the story is just a sidebar to talk about my brother because I loved him so much and just wanted you to know him too.

APPENDIX

List of weapons you can use to get rid of your man.

- Interpret incorrectly; adding to, coming up with your own definition. (Ex. He says, wait; you say no, let's go now.)

- Ignore and accept unacceptable behavior before there is a commitment. (Ex. Overlook red flags. Once he understands that you allow certain behaviors, he realizes you don't have a standard, so you don't care what he does, and he disconnects from you.)

- Practice speaking lowly of him.

- Practice revenge; make sure you always get him back.

- Have a "take over" spirit where you do the leading.

- Disrespect him regularly and minimize or undermine his leadership.

- Talk to outsiders about him and listen to ungodly wisdom.

- Be disloyal to him.

- Smile in his face, knowing you are not going to do a thing he asked.

- Cheat.

- Don't feed him.

- Don't encourage or affirm him.

- Whenever he shows he cares, make sure you make him feel insecure.

- Say **no** to important things.

- Be closed-minded and stubborn.

- Whenever he asks, *"Do you care about me?"* You reply with, *"Of course, but you can do what you wanna do!"* (In other words, I really don't care.)

- Whenever he calls to check on you, make him feel like he's bugging you.

- Ignore his feelings.

- Spend as much money as you possibly can without a care in the world. (Ex. Shop 'til you drop.)

- Move family and friends into your home who cause him to move right on out.

- Let your family and friends borrow whatever they like without his permission.

- Complain whenever opportunity permits.

TitiaOwensBooks.com
- Where you can order books and products.

TitiaOwens.com
- Learn about the many facets of Titia. She has multiple gifts which allow her to serve in various areas.

WhereAreYouOutreach.org
-Our non-profit organization that is a resource provider to the Homeless and those in need.
Donate:
www.PayPal.me/whereareyou

Titia would love for you to send her a pic of yourself with the book in hand. Please post and share the book. You can follow the HOW TO GET RID OF A MAN facebook page.
Email: titiaowens@gmail.com

Drink of choice

CPSIA information can be obtained
at www.ICGtesting.com
Printed in the USA
LVHW041334210822
726126LV00001B/1